Songs from Lovecraft and Others

Songs from Lovecraft and Others

S. T. Joshi

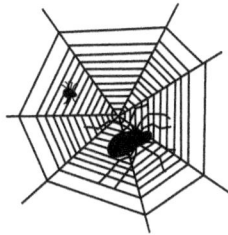

Hippocampus Press

New York

Published by Hippocampus Press
P.O. Box 641, New York, NY 10156.
www.hippocampuspress.com

Cover artwork is *Portrait of a Youth with a Viola da Gamba* (1672) by Jan Verkolje.
Cover design by Daniel V. Sauer, dansauerdesign.com
Hippocampus Press logo designed by Anastasia Damianakos.

First Edition 2022
1 3 5 7 9 8 6 4 2

ISBN 978-1-61498-382-8

CONTENTS

Introduction 7

Songs 11

    Sunset · *H. P. Lovecraft* 13

    Ecstasy · *Clark Ashton Smith* 19

    To Helen · *Edgar Allan Poe* 27

    Continuity · *H. P. Lovecraft* 37

    Non Sum Qualis Eram · *Ernest Dowson* 49

    Ever of You · *George Sterling* 61

    Expectancy · *H. P. Lovecraft* 69

    My Swan Song · *George Sterling* 81

    Background · *H. P. Lovecraft* 91

    Requiescat · *Clark Ashton Smith* 103

    To Science · *George Sterling* 113

    Little Sam Perkins · *H. P. Lovecraft* 125

    A Dirge of Victory · *Lord Dunsany* 133

    Imprisoned · *Mary K. Wilson* 143

Trumpet Concerto in D 149

Texts of the Poems 177

INTRODUCTION

In *What Is Anything? Memoirs of a Life in Lovecraft* (2018), I have recounted my early attempts at musical composition, generally confined to my high school years. Having begun playing the violin at the age of seven or eight, I continued at it until the age of eighteen. At fourteen I made some attempts at composition. Just as, in my nascent literary career, one of my earliest works was a full-scale detective novel, I actually composed a full-length symphony at this time, which I estimated to run to about 25 minutes. It was very poor, of course, and subsequently I composed smaller-scale works—all for strings (although a few for brass and woodwinds) and all in frank imitation of the Baroque composers (chiefly Vivaldi, Corelli, and Handel) I most admired.

Even though I sang in my high school choir in addition to playing in the orchestra, it never occurred to me at that time to compose choral works. My attempts at composition in any event came to an end when I entered Brown University in 1976, since I made a conscious decision to pursue literature rather than music as a career. I did dash off a violin concerto in a few days at the end of my freshman year of college, but it was mediocre and I quickly discarded it. I also set down what I still believe to be an able transcription of Bach's *Italian Concerto* (for harpsichord) as a concerto for violin and strings. (Bach himself clearly modelled the work on the concerti of Vivaldi.)

When I moved to Seattle in late 2001, I soon joined the Northwest Chorale, one of many community choral groups in the city. Under the guidance of its exceptionally talented director, Lynn Hall, I gained a comprehensive understanding of choral music, performing such masterworks as Handel's *Messiah* (which I had performed in high school, both as a tenor and as a violinist), *Requiems* by Mozart, Verdi, Duruflé, and Rutter, Bach's *B Minor Mass,* and many shorter works by contemporary composers. It was the example of these composers—among them Morten Lauridsen, Stephen Paulus, and others—that led me to resume composition, this time for chorus. And it occurred to me that the texts of my compositions could well be taken from the poets I most admired—Edgar Allan Poe, H. P. Lovecraft, Clark Ashton Smith, and George Sterling.

My first work, "Sunset," based on a poem by Lovecraft,[1] was begun in late 2017 and completed in early 2018. I now regard it as somewhat rudimentary, but Mr. Hall thought well enough of it to schedule it for performance at the Northwest Chorale's concert in May 2019. That performance was recorded on video by Greg Lowney, and an audio version of it (prepared by Joshua Rex) is included available for free download at the Hippocampus Press website.[2] I do not have much to say about this piece aside from the fact that I attempted—as I do in all my compositions—to bring out the meaning and significance of the words through musical figures. At times the result may be somewhat naïve word-painting in the

---

1. First published in the *Tryout* (December 1917).
2. Audio files for all the works in this book are located at hippocampuspress.com/other-authors/music/songs-from-lovecraft-and-others-by-s.-t.-joshi.

lomanner of Handel's "All we like sheep" chorus from *Messiah,* but I still find some effectiveness in the process. It is of interest that another composer, Jonathan Adams, has also set "Sunset" to music, and his version could not be more different from mine. Both of them can be seen and heard on YouTube.

Other poems that I've set from Lovecraft were taken mostly from his sonnet cycle *Fungi from Yuggoth,* written mostly in the last week of December 1929 and the first week of January 1930. "Continuity"[3] is the last poem of that cycle, and I have attempted to convey its cosmic message with the use of open chords; other aspects of the poem are more earthly, and in fact reflect a sensitive awareness (rare in his work) of the spiritual value of simple, familiar things. I composed the piece in early 2019; when my friend W. H. Pugmire passed away on March 26, 2019, it seemed appropriate to dedicate my song to him, given what a devoted enthusiast of Lovecraft he was. "Expectancy"[4] is somewhat similar to "Continuity" in its overall thrust, while "Background"[5] is an avowedly autobiographical poem that focuses on Lovecraft's ties to the city that gave him birth (Providence, R.I.)—its topography, its history, and its overall ambiance. As I myself am familiar with the city through six years' residence (1976–82) and many subsequent visits, I found the poem unusually meaningful. The last poem I set from Lovecraft is "Little Sam Perkins,"[6] his poignant elegy to a deceased cat. My own cat, Henry, had passed away not long before I wrote the piece, so it is dedicated to him.

Clark Ashton Smith's "Ecstasy"[7] is one of the poems where he largely eschews the cosmic remoteness of his early work. As it is a frank love elegy (although we do not know to whom it is addressed) with clear sexual imagery, I felt that a lush, languid setting in a lilting 6/8 measure was suitable. "Requiescat"[8] is nominally a dirge (its original title was in fact "Dirge"), but its opening stanzas seem anything but funereal; it is only toward the end that the deathly element enters.

George Sterling's poetry is supremely song-like; he himself published a book of his *Songs* (1916; rev. 1928), in which several of his poems were set to music by Lawrence Zenda (pseudonym of Rosaleine Travis); Sterling composed the music for one of these poems ("Holy River of Sleep"). "Ever of You"[9] struck me as particularly amenable to a musical setting. "To Science"[10] is a bitter atheistic poem, and I felt that a frenetically rapid tempo was needed to bring out the grimness of this work. "My Swan Song"[11] is a poem that was found among Sterling's papers after his suicide in November 1926, and its pensive ruminations on the futility of existence have long attracted me.

Edgar Allan Poe's "To Helen"[12] scarcely requires any discussion, aside from the fact that this is the first of two poems of that title in his corpus, and that it contains those imperishable lines "The glory that was Greece / And the grandeur that was Rome." As a student of classical literature, history, and

---

3. *Fungi from Yuggoth* XXXVI. First published in the *Pioneer* (Summer 1932).

4. *Fungi from Yuggoth* XXVIII. First published in *Fungi from Yuggoth* (1943).

5. *Fungi from Yuggoth* XXX. First published in the *Providence Journal* (16 April 1930).

6. First published in the *Olympian* (Autumn 1940).

7. First published in *Pearson's Magazine* (October 1922); included in Smith's *Ebony and Crystal* (1922).

8. First published in the *Smart Set* (August 1922); included in Smith's *Ebony and Crystal* (1922).

9. First published in Sterling's *Complete Poetry* (Hippocampus Press, 2013). The poem is dated 7 July 1918.

10. First published in the *Sonnet* (July–August 1919).

11. First published in the *San Francisco Call and Post* (8 January 1927).

12. First published in Poe's *Poems* (1831).

philosophy, I found those lines particularly resonant.

A recent composition of mine is a setting of Ernest Dowson's famous poem "Non Sum Qualis Eram Bonae Sub Regno Cynarae."[13] This poem created something of a scandal in its day, as it was obviously addressed to a prostitute, to whom the poet remains "faithful" to the extent of being unable to give his heart fully to any other woman. Strangely, the actual Latin title of the poem (a line from Horace's *Odes*, which translates to "I Am Not as I Was under the Sway of the Good [or perhaps Lovely] Cynara") never appears in the text of the poem, so I have placed those words at the end of my setting. I may note that in classical Latin the name Cynara should be pronounced Kin-AH-rah (the genitive case, Cynarae, as Kin-AH-rye), and that would be my preference for the pronunciation of the name.

My setting of Lord Dunsany's "A Dirge of Victory" aims to bring out the searing ambivalence that the author must have felt at the conclusion of World War I, a conflict in which he served. The poem was published in the London *Times* on Armistice Day 1918—the only poem published in that issue, an indication of the high regard in which Dunsany and his work were regarded at the time.

My setting of "Imprisoned," a poem written by my wife, Mary K. Wilson, may seem inapposite, even jarring, in that it may not convey the horror element of the poem as vividly as it could have; but this was by design. This poem is, in fact, the only explicitly weird poem I have set to music. My decision to use poems of love, philosophical contemplation, and analogous subjects rather than horror or terror has to do with my desire to adhere to Oscar Wilde's old dictum, "The artist is the creator of beautiful things." Contemporary classical music strikes me as being a bit too fond of dissonance and formlessness—to my mind this is not a "beautiful thing." Dissonance should be a spice, not a staple, and that is how I have chosen to compose my pieces.

The piece I have included in the appendix—a trumpet concerto in three movements—is a composition I have been sporadically working on for years, perhaps decades. I believe I wrote the first movement sometime in the 1990s, but I completed it and wrote the other two movements only recently. I include it here merely as an example of the kind of composition—a close (but, I trust, not slavish) imitation of Baroque music—that I attempted from my high school years onward.

Aside from "Sunset," none of these songs have been performed; and, given the pandemic conditions that existed during the composition of most of these pieces, it was impracticable to gather even a small number of choir members for the rehearsal, performance, and recording of the songs. However, my music notation software is capable of producing sound files that play the notes in imitation of the human voice, but without articulating the words; hence, these files have been placed at the Hippocampus Press website for free download. Anyone with even a rudimentary knowledge of music notation should be able to follow the scores of the individual pieces while listening to these sound files, and I hope that listeners will thereby gain at least some semblance of the general nature of these compositions.

I am grateful to my publisher, Derrick Hussey, and our designer, David E. Schultz, for indulging me in the publication of this book.

—S. T. JOSHI

Seattle, Washington
November 2021

---

13. First published in *The Century Guild Hobby Horse*, vol. 6, ed. H. P. Horne (1891); reprinted in Dowson's *Poems* (1902).

SONGS

Sunset

For the Northwest Chorale

H. P. Lovecraft

S. T. Joshi

Andante grazioso

♩ = 70

Soprano:
The cloud-less day is
And in that no - bler,

rich - er at its close;
gent - ler, love - lier light,

Alto:
The cloud-less day is
And in that no - bler,

rich - er at its close;
gent - ler, love - lier light,
The cloud - less
that no - bler

Tenor:
The cloud-less day is rich - er at its close; cloud-less day is
And in that nob - ler, gent-ler, love-lier light, in that no - bler,

rich - er at its close;
gent - ler, love - lier light,
The cloud - less day
that no - bler light,

Bass:
The cloud-less day is
And in that no - bler,

rich - er at its close, The cloud - less day
gent - ler, love - lier light, that no - bler light,

13

7
S.
f
The cloud-less day is rich-er, rich-er, at its close;
that no-bler light, that gent-ler, gent-ler, love-lier light,
A.
f
day is rich-er, rich-er, at its close; A gold-en glo-ry set-tles
light, that gent-ler, gent-ler, love-lier light, the soul to sweet-er, loft-ier
T.
f
is rich-er, rich-er, at its close;
that gent-ler, gent-ler, love-lier light,
B.
f
is rich-er, rich-er, at its close;
that gent-ler, gent-ler, love-lier light,
11
S.
mf
A gold-en glo-ry set-tles on the lea, set-tles,
The soul to sweet-er, loft-ier bliss in-clines; sweet-er,
A.
on the lea; gold-en glo-ry set-tles on the lea, set-tles,
bliss in-clines; soul to sweet-er, loft-ier bliss in-clines; sweet-er,
T.
mf
A gold-en glo-
The soul to sweet-
B.
mf
A gold-en glo-
The soul to sweet-

set-tles set-tles on the lea; Soft, steal-ing shad-ows
sweet-er, loft-ier bliss in - clines; Freed from the noon-day

set - tles set-tles on the lea; Soft,
sweet-er, loft-ier bliss in - clines; Freed

- ry set-tles on the lea, set-tles on the lea; Soft,
- er, loft-ier bliss in - clines; loft-ier bliss in - clines; Freed

- ry set - tles on the lea, set-tles on the lea; Soft,
- er, loft-ier bliss in - clines; loft-ier bliss in - clines; Freed

hint of cool re - pose to mellow-ing land-scape, and to
glare, the fa-voured sight In - creas-ing grace in earth and

steal - ing shad-ows to mellow-ing land-scape, and to
from the noon-day In - creas-ing grace in earth and

steal - ing shad-ows hint of cool re - pose land-scape and to
from the noon-day glare, the fa-voured sight grace in earth and

steal - ing shad-ows hint of cool re - pose land-scape, and to
from the noon-day glare, the fa-voured sight grace in earth and

calm-ing sea, / sky di-vines,   to calm-ing sea / in earth and sky   to calm-ing sea / in earth and sky   calm-ing / sky di -

calm-ing sea, / sky di-vines,   to calm-ing sea / in earth and sky   to calm-ing sea / in earth and sky   calm-ing / sky di -

calming sea / sky di-vines,   to calm-ing sea / in earth and sky   to calm-ing sea, / in earth and sky,   calm-ing / sky di -

calm-ing sea / sky di-vines,   to calm-ing sea / in earth and sky   to calm-ing sea, / in earth and sky,   calm-ing / sky di -

sea. / vines.   But ere the pur - est rad-iance crowns the green,

sea. / vines.   But ere the pur - est

sea. / vines.   But ere the pur - est

sea. / vines.   But ere the pur - est

16   Copyright 2018 by S. T. Joshi

Or fair-est lus - tre fills th'ex-pec-tant grove, The twi-light thick - ens,

rad-iance crowns the green, lus - tre fills th'ex-pec-tant grove,

rad-iance crowns the green, lus - tre fills th'ex-pec-tant grove,

rad-iance crowns the green, lus - tre fills th'ex-pec-tant grove,

and the fleet-ing scene and cresc. _ _ _ _ _ _ _ _ _ _ mf

and the fleet-ing scene the fleet-ing scene the fleet-ing scene the fleet-ing

and the fleet-ing scene the fleet-ing scene the fleet-ing scene the fleet-ing

and the fleeting-scene the fleet-ing scene the fleet-ing scene the fleet-ing

S. leaves but a hal - lowed mem-o - ry mem-o - ry mem-o - ry of

A. scene the fleet-ing scene leaves a hal - lowed mem-o-ry mem-o-ry of

T. scene the fleet-ing scene leaves but a hal - lowed mem-o-ry mem-o-ry of

B. scene the fleet-ing scene leaves a hal - lowed mem-o-ry mem-o-ry of

S. love love love love.

A. love love love love.

T. love love love love.

B. love love.

Ecstasy

Clark Ashton Smith

S. T. Joshi

♩ = 60

Soprano — *mp*
Ah

Alto — *mp*
Ah
I turn me from the
Ache with an ec-sta-

Tenor — *mf*
Blind with your soft - ly fall - en hair,   I turn me from the
Our strain-ing arms that clasp and close   Ache with an ec-sta-

Bass — *mp*

dim.

S.
My lips up - on your
Like burn - ing am - ber

A.
twi-light air;
say that grows,
dim.
My lips up - on your
Like burn - ing am - ber

T.
twi-light air;   And, ah, the word - less tale of love   My lips up - on your
sy that grows,   And pas - sion in our se cret veins,   Like burn - ning am - ber,
dim.

B. — *mf*
And, ah, the word - less tale of love   My lips up - on your
And pas - sion in our se cret veins,   Like burn - ning am - ber,
dim.

19

Lyrics under the first system (measures 10–14):

S.
lips de-clare! Blind with your soft - ly fall - en hair, I turn me from the
glows and glows. Our strain-ing arms that clasp and close Ache with an ec - sta-

A.
lips de-clare! Blind with your soft - ly fall - en hair, I turn me from the
glows and glows. Our strain-ing arms that clasp and close Ache with an ec - sta-

T.
lips de-clare! Blind with your soft - ly fall - en hair, I turn me from the
glows and glows. Our strain-ing arms that clasp and close Ache with an ec - sta-

B.
lips de-clare! Blind with your soft - ly fall - en hair, I turn me from the
glows and glows. Our strain-ing arms that clasp and close Ache with an ec - sta-

Lyrics under the second system (measures 15–):

S.
twi - light air; And, ah, ah, the word - less tale of love My lips
sy that grows, And, ah, ah, And pas - sion in our se - cret veins,

A.
twi - light air; And, ah, ah, the word - less tale of love My lips
sy that grows, And, ah, ah, And pas - sion in our se - cret veins,

T.
twi - light air; ah, ah, the word - less tale of love My lips
sy that grows, ah, ah, And pass - sion in our se - cret veins,

B.
twi - light air; ah, ah, the word - less tale of love My lips
sy that grows, ah, ah, And pas - sion in our se - cret veins,

up - on your lips de-clare! Ah
Like burn - ing am - ber glows.

up - on your lips de-clare High stars are on the shad-ow - y south; Un-
Like burn - ing am - ber glows. This love is sweet to have and hold, Bet-

up - on your lips de-clare! Ah south; Un-
Like burn - ing am - ber glows. hold, Bet-

up - on your lips de-clare! Ah
Like burn - ing am - ber glows.

seen, un-known: the ur - gent drouth Ah
ter than san - dal - wood or gold,

seen, un-known: the ur - gent drouth Ah
ter than san - dal - wood or gold,

Of des-o-late years in one deep kiss Would
Af-ter the bar - ren, bit - ter loves, The

21

Lyrics (Soprano, Alto, Tenor, Bass — measures 31–35):

High stars are on the shad-ow-y south; Un-
This love is sweet to have and hold, Bet-

Bass (measures 31–35):
drain the sweet-ness of your mouth. High stars are on the shad-ow-y south; Un-
mad and mourn-ful loves of old. This love is sweet to have and hold, Bet-

Lyrics (measures 36+):

seen, un-known the ur-gent drouth Of des-o-late years in one deep kiss Would
ter than san-dal-wood or gold, Af-ter the bar-ren, bit-ter loves, The

S.
drain the sweet-ness of your mouth, the sweet the sweet-ness of your mouth, the
mad and mourn-ful loves of old, the mad, the mourn-ful loves of old, the

A.
drain the sweet-ness of your mouth, the sweet the sweet-ness of your mouth, the
mad and mourn-ful loves of old, the mad, the mourn-ful loves of old, the

T.
drain the sweet-ness of your mouth, the sweet the sweet-ness of your mouth, the
mad and mourn-ful loves of old, the mad, the mourn-ful loves of old, the

B.
drain the sweet-ness of your mouth, the sweet the sweet-ness of your mouth, the
mad and mourn-ful loves of old, the mad, the mourn-ful loves of old, the

S.
sweet-ness of your mouth. This love is for-tu-nate and fair, Be-hind its veil of
mourn-ful loves of old.

A.
sweet-ness of your mouth. Ah Be-hind its veil of
mourn-ful loves of old.

T.
sweet-ness of your mouth. Ah
mourn-ful loves of old.

B.
sweet-ness of your mohth. Ah
mourn-ful loves of old.

Lyrics in the music:

S. fall - en hair; This love has soft and cling - ing arms, And a kind bo - som,

A. fall - en hair; This love has soft and cling - ing arms, And a kind bo - som,

S. warm and bare. This love is for - tu-nate and fair, Be-hind its veil of fall - en

A. warm and bare. This love is for - tu-nate and fair, Be-hind its veil of fall - en

T. This love is for - tu-nate and fair, Be-hind its veil of fall - en

B. This love is for - tu-nate and fair, Be-hind its veil of fall - en

Lyrics under the staves:

m. 59:
S./A./T./B.: hair; This love has soft and cling-ing arms, And a kind bo-som, soft and bare,

Dynamics: *f* — *dim.* — — — — — — — — — — — — — *dim.* — — — — — *mp*

m. 62:
S./A./T./B.: soft and bare, soft and bare, a kind bo-som soft and bare.

Dynamics: *dim.* — — — — — — — — — — — *p* — *dim.* — — — — — — — *pp*

To Helen

Edgar Allan Poe

S. T. Joshi

Soprano: Hel-en, thy beau-ty is to me Like those Ni-ce-an barks of yore, That gent-ly o'er a per-fumed sea The wear-y, way-worn wan-d'rer bore To

Alto: Hel-en, thy beau-ty is to me Like those Ni-ce-an barks of yore, That gent-ly o'er a per-fumed sea The wear-y, wa-worn wan-d'rer bore To

Tenor: Hel-en, thy beau-ty is to me Like those Ni-ce-an barks of yore, per-fumed sea The wear-y, way-worn wan-d'rer bore To

Bass: Hel-en, thy beau-ty is to me Like those Ni-ce-an barks of yore, per-fumed sea The wear-y way-worn wan-d'rer bore To

Lyrics from the vocal parts:

System 1 (measures 8–11):
- S: his own na-tive shore. Hel-en, to me
- A: his own na-tive shore. Hel-en, to me
- T: his own na-tive shore. Hel-en, thy beau-ty is to me Like
- B: his own na-tive shore. Hel-en, thy beau-ty is to me Like

System 2 (measures 12–):
- S: of yore, gent-ly gent-ly o'er a per-fumed
- A: of yore, gent-ly gent-ly o'er a per-fumed
- T: those Ni – ce – an barks of yore, That gent-ly, gent-ly o'er a per-fumed
- B: those Ni – ce – an barks of yore, That gent-ly, gent-ly o'er a per-fumed

15
S.
f sea
mp wan-d'rer bore the wan - d'rer bore To
A.
f sea The wear - y, way-worn
mf wan-d'rer bore the wan - d'rer bore To
T.
f sea
mp wan-d'rer bore the wan - d'rer bore To
B.
f sea
mp wan-d'rer bore the wan - d'rer bore To
18
S.
his own na - tive f shore. mp On des - p'rate seas long wont to
A.
his own na - tive f shore. mp On des - p'rate seas long wont to
T.
his own ha - tive f shore.
B.
his own na - tive f shore.

21
S.
cresc.
mf
roam, Thy hy - a-cinth hair, thy
A.
cresc.
mf
roam, Thy hy - a-cinth hair, thy
T.
mp cresc.
mf
On des - p'rate seas long wont to roam, Thy hy - a-cinth hair,
B.
mp cresc.
mf
On des - p'rate seas long wont to roam, Thy hy - a-cinth hair,
23
S.
cresc.
clas - sic face, Thy Nai - ad airs have brought me home,
A.
cresc.
clas - sic face, Thy Nai - ad airs have
T.
cresc.
thy clas - sic face, Thy Nai - ad airs have brought home home,
B.
cresc.
thy classic face, Thy Nai - ad airs have

25
S.
A.
T.
B.
f
brought me home, brought me home,
brought me home, brought me home, brought me home
brought me home, brought me home
brought me home, brought me home, brought me home,
27
dim.
mp
On des-p'rate seas long wont to roam, Thy hy-a-cinth hair,
On des-p'rate seas long wont to roam, Thy hy-a-cinth hair,
On des-p'rate seas long wont to roam, Thy hy-a-cinth
On des-p'rate seas long wont to roam, Thy hy-a-cinth

29
S.
cresc.
mf
thy clas-sic face, Thy Nai - ad airs have brought me home To the
A.
cresc.
mf
thy clas-sic face, Thy Nai - ad airs have brought me home
T.
cresc.
mf
hair, thy clas-sic face, Thy Nai - ad airs have brought me home To the
B.
cresc.
mf
hair, thy clas-sic face, Thy Nai - ad airs have brought me home
32
S.
f
glo - ry that was Greece, The glo - ry
A.
And the grand-eur that was Rome.
T.
f
glo - ry that was Greece, The glo - ry
B.
And the grand-eur that was Rome.

Measure 36:

S. that was Greece, *cresc.* The glo-ry that was Greece,

A. *f* And the grand-eur that was Rome. *cresc.* The glo-ry that was Greece,

T. that was Greece, *cresc.* The glo-ry that was Greece,

B. *f* And the grand-eur that was Rome. *cresc.* The glo-ry that was Greece,

Measure 42:

Meno mosso

S. And the grand-eur that was Rome. *ff* *p* Lo! in yon bril-liant win-dow-

A. And the grand-eur that was Rome. *ff* *p* Lo! in yon bril-liant win-dow-

T. And the grand-eur that was Rome. *ff* *p* Lo! in yon bril-liant win-dow-

B. And the grand-eur that was Rome. *ff* *p* Lo! in yon bril-liant win-dow-niche How stat-ue-like I see thee stand, The a-gate lamp with-in thy hand!

niche How stat-ue-like I see thee stand, The a-gate lamp with-in thy hand!

niche How stat-ue-like I see thee stand, The a-gate lamp with-in thy hand!

niche How stat-ue-like I see thee stand, The a-gate lamp with-in thy hand!

Ah

Ah win-dow-niche Ah

in Lo! in yon bril-liant win-dow - niche How stat-ue - like I see thee

Ah wind-ow-niche Ah stat-ue-like

52
S.
mp
Ah
mf
Ah, Psy-che,
A.
mp
Ah
mf
Ah, Psy-che,
T.
mf
stand, The a-gate lamp with-in thy hand, with - in thy hand!
mf
Ah, Psy-che,
B.
mp
mf
Ah
Ah
Ah, Psy-che,
56
S.
cresc.
f
from the re-gions which are Ho - ly Land, Ho - ly Land, Ho-ly Land!
A.
cresc.
f
from the re-gions which are Ho - ly Land, Ho - ly Land, Ho-ly
T.
cresc.
f
from the re-gions which are Ho - ly Land, Ho - ly Land, Ho-ly
B.
cresc.
f
from the re-gions which are Ho - ly Land, Ho - ly Land, Ho-ly Land!

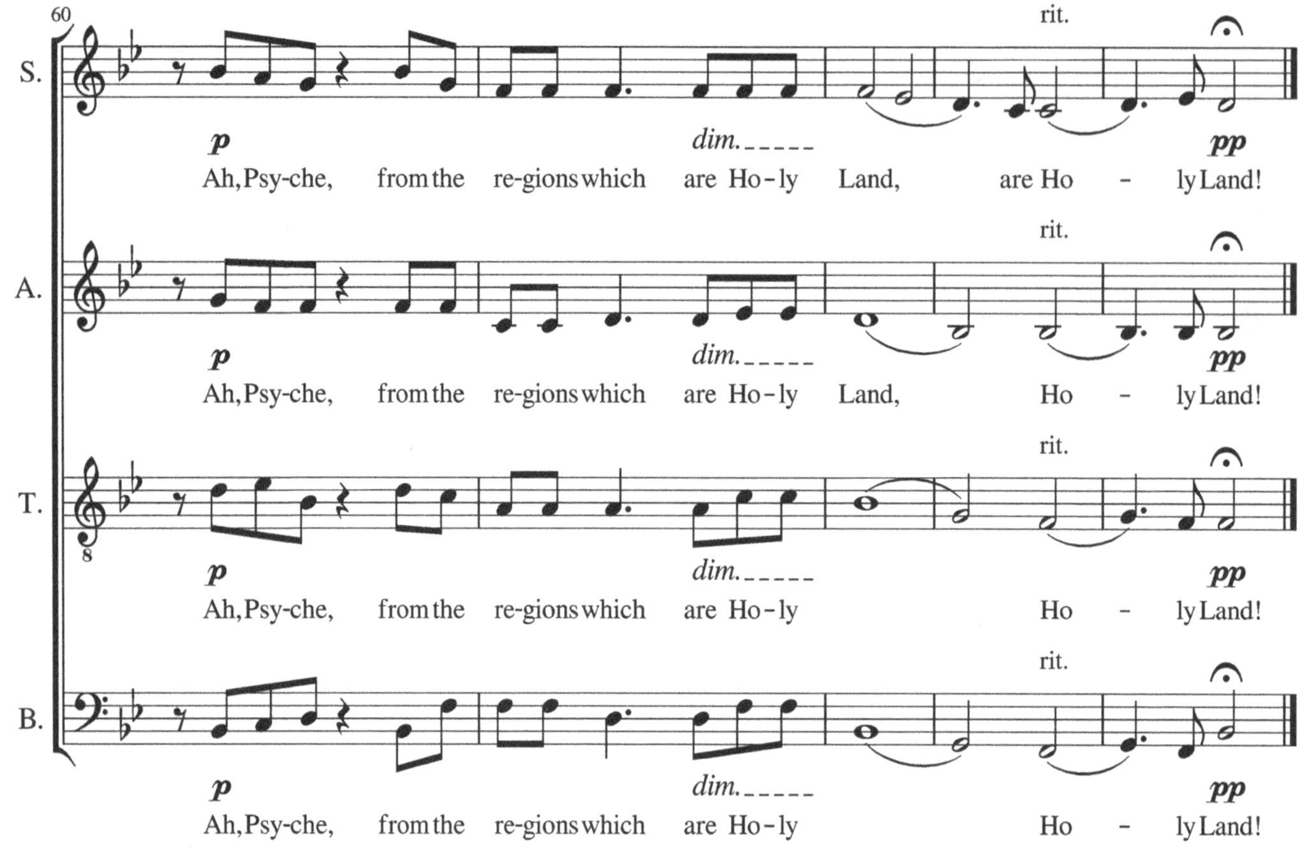
60
rit.
S.
p
dim.
pp
Ah, Psy-che, from the re-gions which are Ho-ly Land, are Ho - ly Land!
A.
p
dim.
pp
Ah, Psy-che, from the re-gions which are Ho-ly Land, Ho - ly Land!
T.
p
dim.
pp
Ah, Psy-che, from the re-gions which are Ho-ly Ho - ly Land!
B.
p
dim.
pp
Ah, Psy-che, from the re-gions which are Ho-ly Ho - ly Land!

Continuity

To the memory of W. H. Pugmire

H. P. Lovecraft

S. T. Joshi

Andante tranquillo ♩ = 60

Soprano — *p* Ah

Alto — *p* Ah

Tenor — *mp* There is in cer-tain an-cient things a trace of some dim

Bass — *p* Ah

S. — *mp* There is in cer-tain an-cient

A. — *mp* There is in cer-tain an-cient

T. — es - sence, more than form or weight; *mp* There is in cer - tain

B. — *mp* There is in cer - tain

Lyrics under the music:

Soprano (mm. 7–9): things a trace of some dim es-sence, more than form or weight,

Alto (mm. 7–9): things a trace of some dim es-sence, more than form or weight,

Tenor (mm. 7–9): an-cient things a trace form or weight

Bass (mm. 7–9): an-cient things a trace form or weight,

Soprano (mm. 10–): form or weight; a ten-uous ae-ther, in – de – ter – mi-nate,

Alto (mm. 10–): form or weight; a ten-uous ae-ther, in – de – ter – mi-nate,

Tenor (mm. 10–): form or weight; a ten – uous ae – ther,

Bass (mm. 10–): form or weight; a ten – uous ae – ther,

13
S.
A.
T.
B.
cresc.
in - de - ter - mi-nate, in - de - ter - mi-nate, a
mf
cresc.
in - de - ter - mi-nate, in - de - ter - mi-nate, a
mf
cresc.
in - de - ter - mi - nate, in - de - ter - mi-
mf
cresc.
in - de - ter - mi-nate, in - de -
mf
15
ten-uous ae - ther, in - de - ter - mi-nate, yet linked with all the laws of time and
dim.
mp
ten-uous ae - ther, in - de - ter - mi-nate, ah
dim.
p
nate, in - de - ter - mi-nate, ah
dim.
p
ter - mi-nate, in - de - ter - mi-nate, ah
dim.
p

Lyrics from the choral parts:

S. space, of time and space. ah with all the laws of time and

A. with all the laws of time and

T. with all the laws of time and space, ah

B. with all the laws of time and space, ah

S. space, let linked with all the laws of time and space.

A. space, yet linked with all the laws of time and space,

T. yet linked with all the laws of time and space,

B. yet linked with all the laws of time and space,

S. with all the laws of time and space. ah con-ti-

A. ah A faint veiled sign of con-ti-nu-i-ties

T. ah ah con-ti-

B. ah ah con-ti-

S. nu-i-ties A faint, veiled sign of

A. that out-ward eyes can nev-er quite des-cry; A faint, veiled sign of

T. nu-i-ties A faint, veiled sign of

B. nu-i-ties A faint, veiled sign of

41

33
S.
cresc.
f
mf
con-ti-nu - i-ties that out-ward eyes can nev-er quite des-cry;
ah
A.
cresc.
f
mf
con-ti - ties that out-ward eyes can nev-er quite des-cry;
ah
T.
cresc.
f
mf
con-ti-nu - i-ties that out-ward eyes can nev-er quite des-cry;
ah
B.
cresc.
f
con-ti-nu - i-ties that out-ward eyes can nev-er quite des-cry;
of locked di-men-sions
37
S.
har - b'ring years gone by
A.
har - b'ring years gone by,
har - b'ring years gone
T.
har - b'ring years gone by,
B.
har - b'ring years gone by
har - b'ring go ne

S. **dim.** _ _ _ _ _ _ _ _ _ _ **mp** **cresc.** _ _ _ _ _ _ _ _
and out of reach ex - cept for hid - den keys, of locked

A. **dim.** _ _ _ _ _ _ _ _ _ _ **mp** **cresc.** _ _ _ _ _ _ _ _
by, and out of reach ex - cept for hid - den keys, of locked di -

T. **dim.** _ _ _ _ _ _ _ **mp** **cresc.** _ _ _ _ _ _ _ _
and out of reach ex - cept for hid - den keys, of locked di -

B. **dim.** _ _ _ _ _ _ _ **mp** **cresc.** _ _ _ _ _ _ _ _
by and out of reach ex - cept for hid - den keys, of locked di -

rit.

S. **mf** **cresc.** _ _ _ _ _ _ _ _ _ _ _ _ _ _
di-men - sions har-b'ring years gone by, and out of reach ex-cept for hid-den keys, hid - den

rit.

A. **mf** **cresc.** _ _ _ _ _ _ _ _ _ _ _ _ _ _ .
mcn sions har-b'ring years gone by, and out of reach ex-cept for hid-den keys, hid-den

rit.

T. **mf** **cresc.** _ _ _ _ _ _ _ _ _ _ _ _ _ _
men - sions har - b'ring years gone by, and out of reach ex - cept for hid-den keys, hid-den

rit.

B. **mf** **cresc.** _ _ _ _ _ _ _ _ _ _ _ _ _ _
men - sions har - b'ring years gone by, and out of reach ex - cept for hid-den keys, hid-den

43

S.

ff *mp*
keys. ah

A.

ff *mp*
keys. ah

T.

ff *mp*
keys. ah

B.

ff *mf*
keys. It moves me most when slant-ing sun-beams glow on old farm build-ings

S.

A.

T.

mp
It moves me most when slant - ing sun - beams

B.

mp
set a - gainst a hill, It moves me most when slant - ing sun - beams

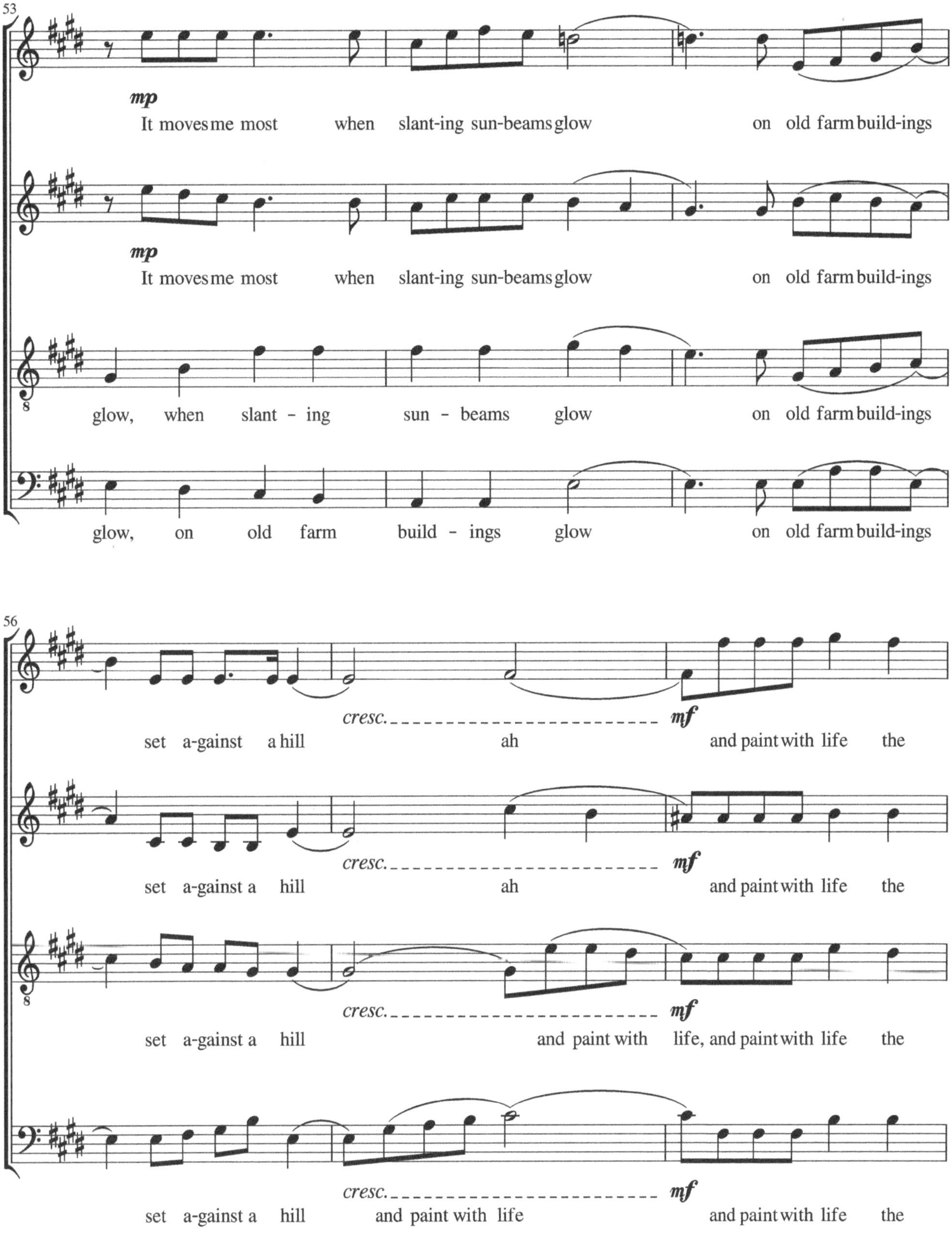

53
S.
mp
It moves me most when slant-ing sun-beams glow on old farm build-ings
A.
mp
It moves me most when slant-ing sun-beams glow on old farm build-ings
T.
glow, when slant - ing sun - beams glow on old farm build-ings
B.
glow, on old farm build - ings glow on old farm build-ings
56
S.
cresc. mf
set a-gainst a hill ah and paint with life the
A.
cresc. mf
set a-gainst a hill ah and paint with life the
T.
cresc. mf
set a-gainst a hill and paint with life, and paint with life the
B.
cresc. mf
set a-gainst a hill and paint with life and paint with life the

shapes which lin-ger still from cen-t'ries less a dream than this we know, from

shapes which lin-ger still from cen-t'ries less a dream than this we know, from

shapes which lin-ger still from cen-t'ries less a dream than this we know, from

shapes which lin-ger still from cen-t'ries less a dream than this we know, from

cen-t'ries less a dream than this we know. Ah

cen-t'ries less a dream than this we know. Ah

cen-t'ries less a dream than this we know. In that strange light I feel I

cen-t'ries less a dream than this we know. Ah

68
S.
A.
T.
B.
f
In that strange light I feel I
f
In that strange light I feel I
am not far from the fixt mass whose sides the a - ges are.
f
In that strange light I feel I
f
In that strange light I feel I
72
cresc.
am not far from the fixt mass whose sides the a-ges are.
ff
Ah
cresc.
am not far from the fixt mass whose sides the a-ges are.
ff
Ah
cresc.
am not far from the fixt mass whose sides the a-ges are.
ff
whose sides the a - ges are.
cresc.
am not far from the fixt mass whose sides the a-ges are.
ff
Ah

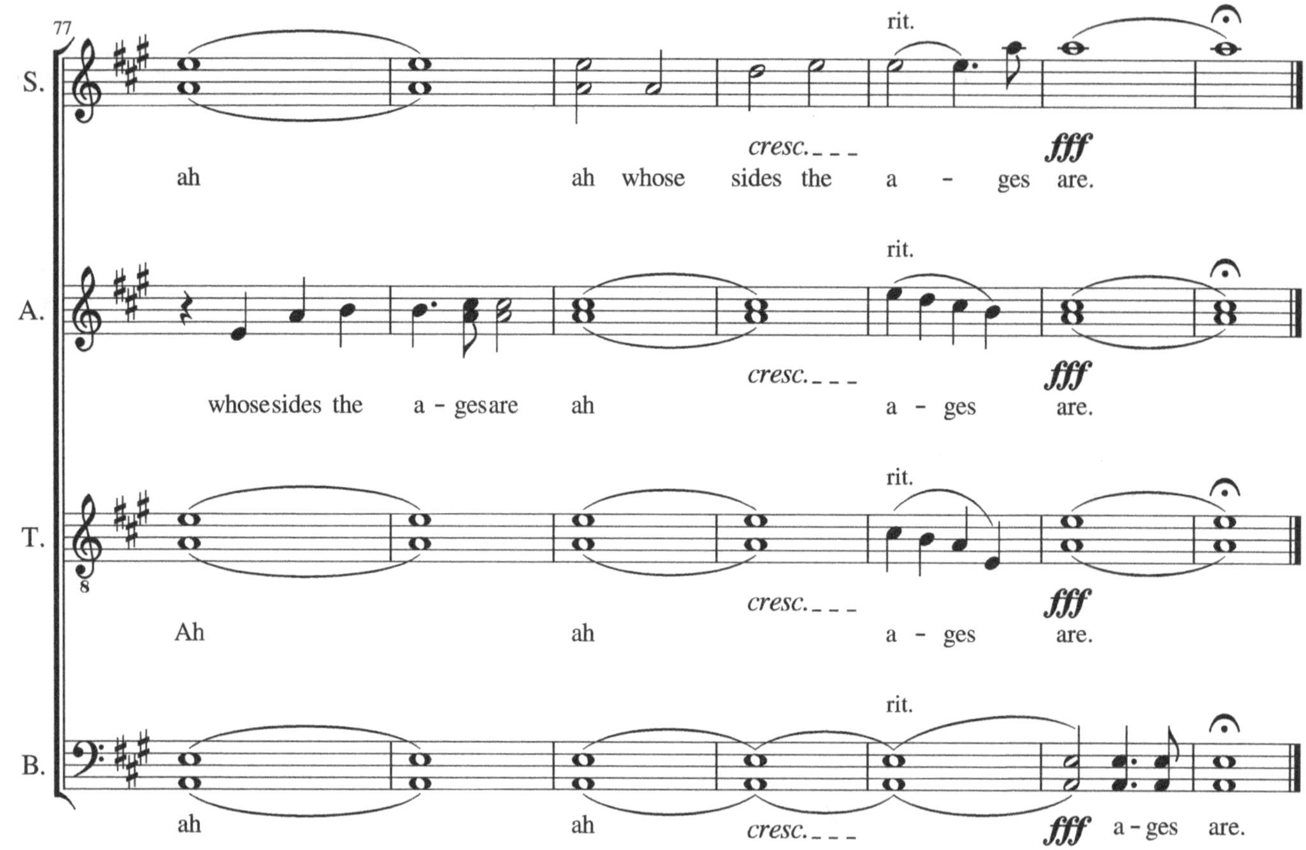
77
S.
rit.
cresc.
fff
ah ah whose sides the a - ges are.
A.
rit.
cresc.
fff
whose sides the a - ges are ah a - ges are.
T.
rit.
cresc.
fff
Ah ah a - ges are.
B.
rit.
ah ah cresc.
fff a - ges are.

Non Sum Qualis Eram

Ernest Dowson

S. T. Joshi

♩ = 60

Soprano

p
Last night, ah, yes-ter-night, be-twixt her lips and mine There
All night up - on mine heart I felt her warm heart beat, Night -

Alto

p
Last night, ah, yes-ter-night, lips and mine There
All night up - on mine heart warm heart beat, Night -

Tenor

p
Last night, ah, yes-ter-night, lips and mine There
All night up - on mine heart warm heart beat, Night -

Bass

p
Last night, ah, yes-ter-night, lips and mine There
All night up - on mine heart warm heart beat, Night -

S.

mp *cresc.* _ _ _ _ _ _ _ _ _ _ *mf*
fell thy sha-dow Cy - na - ra, Cy - na - ra!
long with - in mine arms in love

A.

mp *cresc.* _ _ _ _ _ _ *mf*
fell thy sha-dow Cy - na - ra, Cy - na - ra!
long with - in mine arms in love

T.

mp *cresc.* _ _ _ _ _ _ _ _ *mf* *mp*
fell thy sha-dow Cy - na - ra, Cy - na - ra! Last night, ah, yes-ter-night,
long with - in mine arms in love All night up - on mine heart

B.

mp *cresc.* _ _ _ _ _ _ _ _ _ _ *mp*
fell thy sha-dow Cy - na - ra, Cy - na - ra! Last night, ah, yes-ter-night,
long with - in mine arms in love All night up - on mine heart

49

S.
There fell thy sha - dow, Cy - na - ra! Cy - mine
Night-long with - in mine arms mine

A.
There fell thy sha - dow, Cy - na - ra!
Night-long with - in mine arms

T.
be - twixt her lips and mine sha - dow, Cy - na - ra!
I felt her warm heart beat, with - in mine arms

B.
be - twixt her lips and mine sha - dow, Cy - na - ra!
I felt her warm heart beat, with - in mine arms

S.
na - ra! thy breath was shed Up - on my soul be - tween the kiss - es, the kiss -
arms mine arms in love Sure - ly the kiss - es of her bought red mouth were

A.
Ah kiss - es, the kiss -
Ah bought red mouth were

T.
Ah kiss - es, the kiss -
Ah bought red mouth were

B.
Ah kiss - es, the kiss -
Ah bought red mouth were

51

S.

A.

T.

B.

and the wine; And I was des-o-late and sick of an old pas - sion,
were   sweet; But I was des-o-late and sick of an old pass - ion,

and the wine; And I was des-o-late and sick of an old pas - sion,
were   sweet; But I was des-o-late and sick of an old pas - sion,

and the wine; And I was des-o-late and sick of an old pas - sion, Yea, I was des-o -
were   sweet; But I was des-o-late and sick of an old pas - sion, When I a-woke and

and the wine; And I was des-o-late and sick of an old pas - sion, Yea, I was des-o -
But I was des-o-late and sick of an old pas - sion, When I a-woke and

S.

A.

T.

B.

Yea, I was des - o - late   and bowed   my head, and bowed   my head,
When I a - woke and found   the dawn   was gray,   the dawn   was gray:

Yea, I was des - o - late   and bowed   my head, and bowed   my head:
When I a - woke and found   the dawn   was gray,   the dawn   was gray:

late   and bowed my   head: And bowed   my head:
found   the dawn was   gray: the dawn   was gray:

late   and bowed my   head: And bowed   my head:
found   the dawn was   gray: the dawn   was gray:

Lyrics (Soprano, Alto, Tenor, Bass):
I have been faith-ful to thee, Cy-na-ra! Cy-na-ra! in my fash - ion.
I have been faith-ful to thee, Cy-na-ra! Cy-na-ra! in my fash - ion.

I have for-got much, Cy - na - ra! gone with the wind, the wind, the wind,

S. gone with the wind, Flung ro - ses, ro-ses ri - ot - ous - ly with the throng,

A. wind, gone with the wind, Flung ro ses with the throng,

T. wind, gone with the wind, Flung ro - ses, ro-ses ri - ot - ous - ly with the throng,

B. gone with the wind, Flung ro - ses, ro-ses ri - ot - ous - ly with the thiong,

S. *mp* *mp* *cresc.* _ _ _ _ _ _ _ _ _ _ _ _ _ _ _ _ _ _
Danc-ing, to put thy pale, lost li - lies out of

A. *mp* *mp* *cresc.* _ _ _ _ _ _ _ _ _ _ _ _ _ _ _ _ _
Danc-ing, to put thy pale, lost li - lies out of

T. *mp* *cresc.* _ _ _ _ _ _ _ _ _ _ _ _ _ _ _
Danc-ing to put thy pale, lost li - lies out of mind; put thy pale, lost li - lies out of

B. *mp* *mp* *cresc.* _ _ _ _ _ _ _ _ _ _ _ _ _ _ _ _ _
Danc-ing, to put thy pale, lost li - lies out of

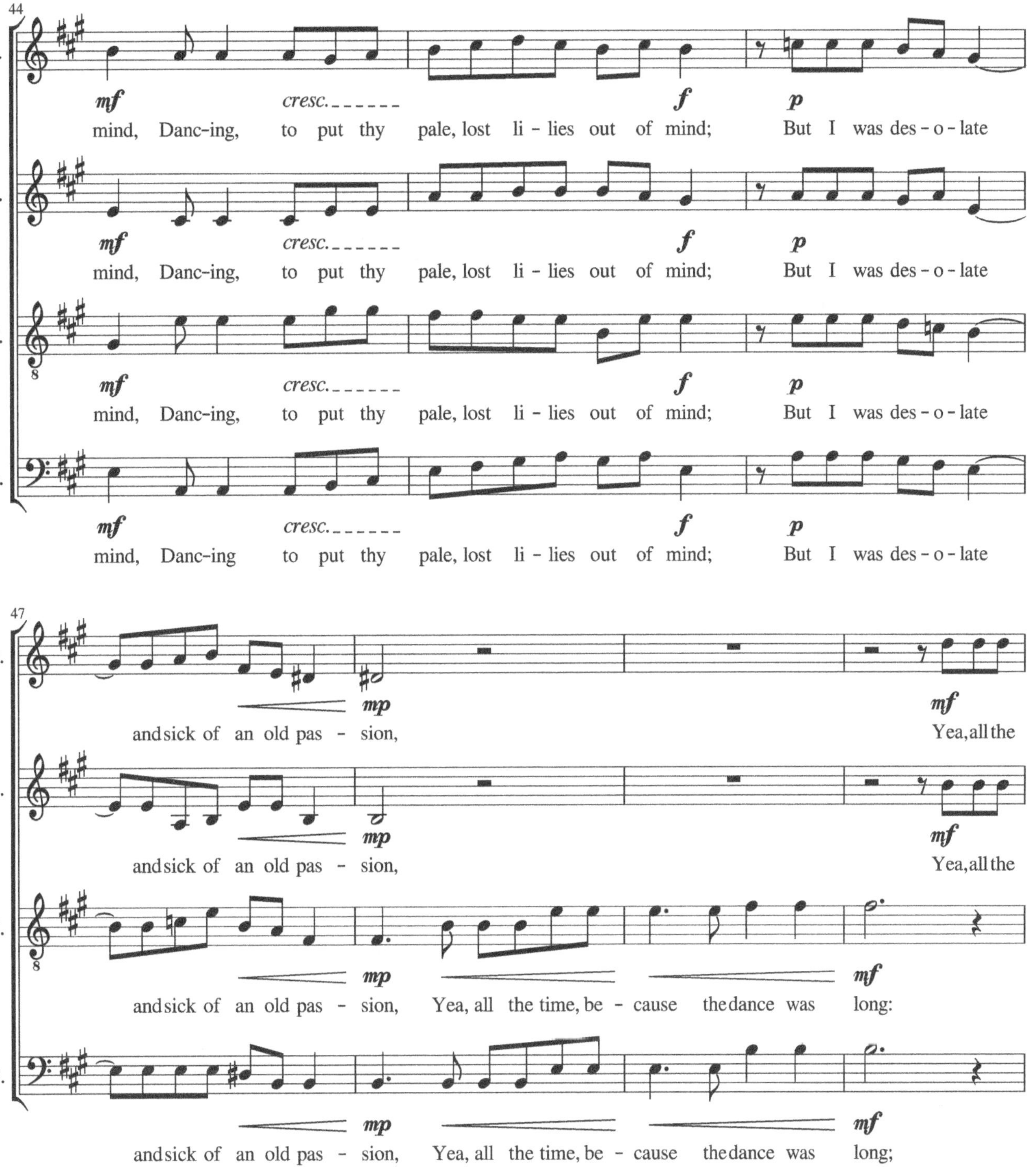

44
S.
A.
T.
B.
mf
cresc.
f
p
mind, Danc-ing, to put thy pale, lost li - lies out of mind; But I was des - o - late
mind, Danc-ing, to put thy pale, lost li - lies out of mind; But I was des - o - late
mind, Danc-ing, to put thy pale, lost li - lies out of mind; But I was des - o - late
mind, Danc-ing to put thy pale, lost li - lies out of mind; But I was des - o - late
47
mp
mf
and sick of an old pas - sion, Yea, all the
and sick of an old pas - sion, Yea, all the
and sick of an old pas - sion, Yea, all the time, be - cause the dance was long:
and sick of an old pas - sion, Yea, all the time, be - cause the dance was long;

Lyrics under the staves:

S., A., T., B. (measure 51):
time, be-cause the dance was long: I have been faith-ful to thee, Cy-na-ra! Cy-na-ra!

S., A. (measure 56):
in my fash-ion. I cried for mad-der mu-sic and for strong-er wine,

T., B. (measure 56):
in my fash-ion. I cried for mad-der mu-sic and for strong-er wine, strong-er

Lyrics under the staves:

Measures 59–62:

S. strong-er wine, strong-er wine,

A. strong-er wine, strong-er wine,

T. wine, strong-er wine, But when the feast is fin - ished and the lamps ex - pire,

B. wine, strong-er wine,

Measures 63 onward:

S. But when the feast is fin - ished and the lamps ex - pire, Then falls thy shad-ow, Cy-na - ra!

A. But when the feast is fin - ished and the lamps ex - pire, ex-pire, Then falls thy shad - ow, Cy-na -

T. Ah   ex-pire, Then falls thy shad - ow, Cy-na -

B. Ah   Then falls thy shad - ow, Cy-na -

67
S.
the night is thine; But I was des-o-late and sick of an old pas - sion,
A.
ra! the night is thine; But I was des-o-late and sick of an old pas - sion,
T.
ra! the night is thine; But I was des-o-late and sick of an old pas - sion, Yea, hun-gry for the
B.
ra! the night is thine; But I was des-o-late and sick of an old pas - sion, Yea, hun-gry for the
mf
p
mp
71
Yea, hun-gry for the lips of my de-sire: I have been faith-ful to thee,
lips of my de - sire: for the lips of my de-sire: I have been fiath-ful to thee,
mf
cresc.
f
mp

76
S.
A.
T.
B.
mf
dim.
p
Cy-na-ra! in my fash-ion, my fash-ion, in my fash - ion.
Cy - na-ra! in my fash-ion, fash-ion, in my fash - ion.
f
Cy - na-ra! in my fash-ion, fash-ion, in my fash - ion. Non sum qual-is e-ram
Cy - na-ra! in my fash-ion, my fash-ion, in my fash - ion.
82
Non sum qual-is e-ram bo-nae sub reg-no Cy-na rae.
Non sum qual-is e-ram bo-nae sub reg-no Cy - na rae.
bo-nae sub reg-no Cy-na rae. Non sum qual-is e-ram bo-nae sub reg-no Cy - na rae.
Non sum qual-is e-ram bo-nae sub reg-no Cy-na rae.

89
S.
mf
mp
cresc.
Non sum qual-is e-ram bo-nae sub reg - no Cy-na - rae, Non sum
A.
mf
p
cresc.
Non sum qual-is e-ram bo-nae sub reg - no Cy - na - rae. Cy-na-rae, Cy-na-rae,
T.
mf
p
cresc.
Non sum qual-is e-ram bo-nae sub reg - no Cy - na - rae. Cy-na-rae, Cy-na-rae,
B.
mf
p
cresc.
Non sum qual-is e-ram bo-nae sub reg - no Cy - na - rae. Cy-na-rae, Cy-na-rae,
95
S.
mf
dim.
pp
Non sum qual-is e-ram bo-nae sub reg-no Cy - na - rae.
A.
mp
dim.
pp
Cy - na-rae, Cy-na - rae, e - ram Cy - na - rae.
T.
mp
dim.
pp
Cy - na-rae, Cy-na - rae, e - ram Cy - na - rae.
B.
mp
dim.
pp
Cy - na-rae, Cy-na - rae, e - ram Cy - na - rae.

Ever of You

George Sterling

S. T. Joshi

Soprano: Ev - er of you, with heart your heart un - fold - ing, Ev - er of you, as

Alto: Ev - er of you, with heart your heart un - fold - ing, Ev - er of you, as

Tenor: Ev - er   Ev - er

Bass: Ev - er   Ev - er

S.: Love our fate is mold - ing, Ev - er of you, whose love has no with - hold - ing,

A.: Love our fate is mold - ing, Ev - er of you, whose love has no with - hold - ing,

T.: Ev - er of you, whose love has no with - hold - ing,

B.: Ev - er of you, whose love has no with - hold - ing,

61

Are all my dreams, are all my dreams. Un-der

Are all my dreams, are all my dreams. Un-der

Are all my dreams, are all my dreams. Un-der the fire of si - lent plan-ets burn-ing,

Are all my dreams, are all my dreams. Un-der the fire of si - lent plan-ets burn-ing,

Un - der   Un-der the qui - et

Un - der   Un-der the qui - et

Un - der the snows of cloud - y dawns re - turn - ing, Un-der the qui - et

Un - der the snows of cloud - y dawns re - turn - ing, Un-der the qui - et

S. noons that know my yearn - ing, I clasp my dreams, I clasp my dreams. _mf_

A. noons that know my yearn - ing, I clasp my dreams, I clasp my dreams. _mf_

T. noons that know my yearn - ing, I clasp my dreams, I clasp my dreams. _mf_

B. noons that know my yearn - ing, I clasp my dreams, I clasp my dreams. _mf_

meno mosso

S. _p_ Ev-er of you, with heart your heart un - fold-ing, Ev-er of you, as Love our fate is

A. _p_ Ev-er of you, with heart your heart un - fold-ing, Ev-er of you, as Love our fate is

T. _p_ Ev-er of you, with heart your heart un - fold-ing, Ev-er of you, as Love our fate is

B. _p_ Ev-er of you, with heart your heart un - fold-ing, Ev-er of you, as Love our fate is

S. mold-ing, Ev-er of you, whose love has no with-hold-ing, Are all my dreams, are

A. mold-ing, Ev-er of you, whose love has no with-hold-ing, Are all my dreams, are

T. mold-ing, Ev-er of you, whose love has no with-hold-ing, Are all my dreams, are

B. mold-ing, Ev-er of you, whose love has no with-hold-ing, Are all my dreams, re

S. all my dreams. Un-der the fire of si-lent plan-ets burn-ing, Un-der the snows of

A. all my dreams. Un-der the fire of si-lent plan-ets burn-ing, Un-der the snows of

T. all my dreams. Un-der the fire of si-lent plan-ets burn-ing, Un-der the snows of

B. all my dreams. Un-der the fire of si-lent plan-ets burn-ing, Un-der the snows of

64   Copyright 2019 by S. T. Joshi

S. cloud-y dawns re-turn-ing, Un-der the qui-et noons that know my yearn-ing,

A. cloud-y dawns re-turn-ing, Un-der the qui-et noons that know my yearn-ing,

T. cloud-y dawns re-turn-ing, Un-der the qui-et noons that know my yearn-ing,

B. cloud-y dawns re-turn-ing, Un-der the qui-et noons that know my yearn-ing,

Tempo 1

S. I clasp my dreams, I clasp my dreams. Ev-er of you, in beau-ty un-for-

A. I clasp my dreams, I clasp my dreams. Ev-er of you, in beau-ty un-for-

T. I clasp my dreams, I clasp my dreams. Ev-er of you, in beau-ty un-for-

B. I clasp my dreams, I clasp my dreams. Ev-er of you, in beau-ty un-for-sa - king, Ev - er of you, for touch of tears a - wa - king, Ev - er of you, al -

sa - king, Ev - er of you, for touch of tears a - wa - king, Ev - er of you, al -

sa - king, Ev - er of you, for touch of tears a - wa - king, Ev - er of you, al -

sa - king, Ev - er of you, for touch of tears a - wa - king, Ev - er of you, al -

though the heart be break-ing, Are all my dreams, are all my dreams, Are all my

though the heart be break-ing, Are all my dreams, are all my dreams, Are all my

though the heart be break-ing, Are all my dreams, are all my dreams, Are all my

though the heart be break-ing, Are all my dreams, are all my dreams, Are all my

S.

f   *cresc.*_ _ _ _ _ _   *ff*

dreams,   Are   all   my   dreams,   my   dreams,   my   dreams,   my   dreams.

A.

f   *cresc.*_ _ _ _ _ _   *ff*

dreams,   Are   all   my   dreams,   my   dreams,   my   dreams,   my   dreams.

T.

f   *cresc.*_ _ _ _ _ _   *ff*

dreams,   Are   all   my   dreams,   my   dreams,   my   dreams,   my   dreams.

B.

f   *cresc.*_ _ _ _ _ _   *ff*

dreams,   Are   all   my   dreams,   my   dreams,   my   dreams,   my   dreams.

Expectancy

H. P. Lovecraft

S. T. Joshi

♩ = 70

Soprano

mp

I can-not tell why some things hold for me

cresc.

Alto

p

Ah

Tenor

p

Ah

Bass

p

Ah

S.

sense of un-plumbed mar-vels to be-fall,

A.

mp

I can-not tell why something hold for me

T.

mp

I can-not tell why something hold for me

B.

mp

I can-not tell why something hold for me

8
S.
mp
cresc.
Or of a rift, or of a
A.
cresc.
cresc.
A sense of un-plumbed mar-vels to be-fall, Or of a rift
T.
cresc.
cresc.
A sense of un-plumbed mar-vels to be-fall, Or of a rift
B.
cresc.
cresc.
A sense of un-plumbed mar-vels to be-fall, Or of a rift
12
S.
f
dim.
p
rift in the ho - ri-on's wall, or of a rift in the ho-ri-zon's wall
A.
f
dim.
p
in the ho - ri-zon's wall, in the ho-ri-zon's wall, ho-ri-zon's
T.
f
dim.
p
in the ho - ri-zon's wall, in the ho-ri-zon's wall, ho-ri-zon's
B.
f
dim.
p
in the ho - ri-zon's wall, inh the ho-ri-zon's wall

71

S.
mf mp p mp
gods can be,   to worlds where on-ly   gods can be.   There is a breath-less,

A.
mf mp p mp
gods can be,   where   gods   can   be.   There is a breath-less,

T.
mf mp p mp
gods can be,   where   gods   can   be.   There is a breath-less,

B.
mf mp p mp
gods can be,   where   gods   can   be.   There is a breath-less,

S.
cresc. _ _ _ _ _ _ _ _   f
vague ex-pec-tan-cy,   As of vast an-cient pomps   I   half re-call,

A.
cresc. _ _ _ _ _ _ _ _   f
vague es-pec-tan-cy,   As of vast an-cient pomps   I   half re-call,   half re-

T.
cresc. _ _ _ _ _ _ _ _   f
vague ex-pec-tan-cy,   As of vast an-cient pomps   I   half re-call,   half re-

B.
cresc. _ _ _ _ _ _ _ _   f
vague ex-pec-tan-cy,   As of vast an-cient pomps   I   half re-call,   half re-

S. un-cor-por - e - al,

A. call, un-cor-por - e - al, Ec-sta-cy -

T. call, Or wild ad - ven-tures, un-cor-por - e - al, Ec-sta-cy -

B. call,

S. There is a breathless,

A. fraught, and as a day-dream free. breath-less, breath-less,

T. fraught, and as a day-dream free. breath-less, breath-less,

B. There is a breath-less,

S. vague ex-pec-tan-cy, As of vast an cient pomps I half re-

A. ex-pec-tan-cy, As of vast an cient pomps I half re-

T. ex-pec-tan-cy, As of vast an cient pomps I half re-

B. vague ex-pec-tan-cy, As of vast an cient pomps I half re-

S. call, Or wild ad-ven-tures, un-cor-por-e-al, Ec-sta-sy-fraught,

A. call, Or wild ad-ven-tures, un-cor-por-e-al, Ec-sta-sy-fraught,

T. call, Or wild ad-ven-tures, un-cor-por-e-al, Ec-sta-sy-fraught,

B. call, Or wild ad-ven-tures, un-cor-por-e-al, Ec-sta-sy-fraught,

51
S.
A.
T.
B.
p
cresc.
and as a day-dream free, day-dream free, day-dream free, day-dream
day-dream free, day-dream free, day-dream free, day-dream
55
f
mp
free, day-dream free. Ah
It is in sun-sets and strange ci - ty spires, Old vil-la-ges

S. It is in sun-sets and strange ci - ty

A. It is in sun-sets and strange ci - ty

T. and woods and mis - ty downs, It is in sun-sets and strange ci - ty

B. It is in sun-sets and strange ci - ty

S. spires, Old vil-la-ges and woods and mis-ty downs, South winds, the

A. spires, Old vil-la-ges and woods and mis-ty downs, South winds, the

T. spires, Old vil-la-ges and woods and mis-ty downs, South winds,

B. spires, Old vil-la-ges and woods and mis-ty downs, South winds,

S. sea, low hills, and light-ed towns,

A. sea, low hills, and light-ed towns,

T. the sea, low hills, and light-ed towns, Old gar-dens, half-heard

B. the sea, low hills, and light-ed towns,

S. Old gar-dens half-heard songs, and the moon's

T. songs, and the moon's fires.

Soprano (m. 76): fires. But though its lure a-lone makes life worth liv-ing, None gains or guess-es what it

Alto (m. 76): *p* Ah

Tenor (m. 76): *p* Ah

Bass (m. 76): *p* Ah

Soprano (m. 80): hints at giv-ing. *mp*

Alto (m. 80): *mp* But though its lure a – lone makes life worth liv – ing, *cresc.*

Tenor (m. 80): *mp* But though its lure a – lone makes life worth liv – ing, *cresc.*

Bass (m. 80): *mp* But though its lure a – lone makes life worth liv – ing, *cresc.*

83
S.
A.
T.
B.
mp
None gains
dim.
None gains or guess - es what it hints at giv - ing,
None gains or
86
rit.
cresc.
mf
p
pp
or guess-es what it hints at giv-ing, what it hints at giv - ing.
nor guess-es what it hints at giv-ing, what it hints at giv - ing.
guess-es what it hints at giv-ing, what it hints at giv - ing.

My Swan Song

George Sterling

S. T. Joshi

Andante mesto ♩ = 60

Soprano

mp

Has man the right To die and dis - ap-pear,

Alto

mp

Has man the right To die and dis - ap-pear

Tenor

mp

Has man the right To die and dis - ap-pear, When

Bass

mp

Has man the right To die and dis - ap-pear,

S.

p *cresc.*

When he has lost the fight? Has man the right,

A.

p *cresc.*

When he has lost the fight? Has man the right

T.

p *cresc.*

he has lost the fight? Has man the

B.

p lost the fight? Has

Has man the right To die and dis - ap - pear, When he has lost the fight?

Has man the right To die and dis - ap - pear, When he has lost the fight, lost the

right, the right To die and dis - ap - pear When he has lost the fight, lost the

man the right, the right To die and dis - ap - pear, When he has lost the fight, lost the

To sev - er with-out fear

fight? To sev-er with-out fear The irk-some bonds of life,

To sev - er with-out fear

The irk-some bonds fo life

S. To sev-er with-out fear The irk-some bonds of life,

A. To sev-er with-out fear The irk-some bonds of life,

T. To sev-er with-out fear The irk-some bonds of life,

B. When he is tired of strife? To sev-er with-out fear The irk-some bonds of life,

S. When he is tired of strife? When he is tired of strife? May he not seek, if

A. When he is tired of strife? When he is tired of strife? May he not seek, if

T. When he is tired of strife? When he is tired of strife? May he not

B. When he is tired of strife, When he is tired of strife? May he not

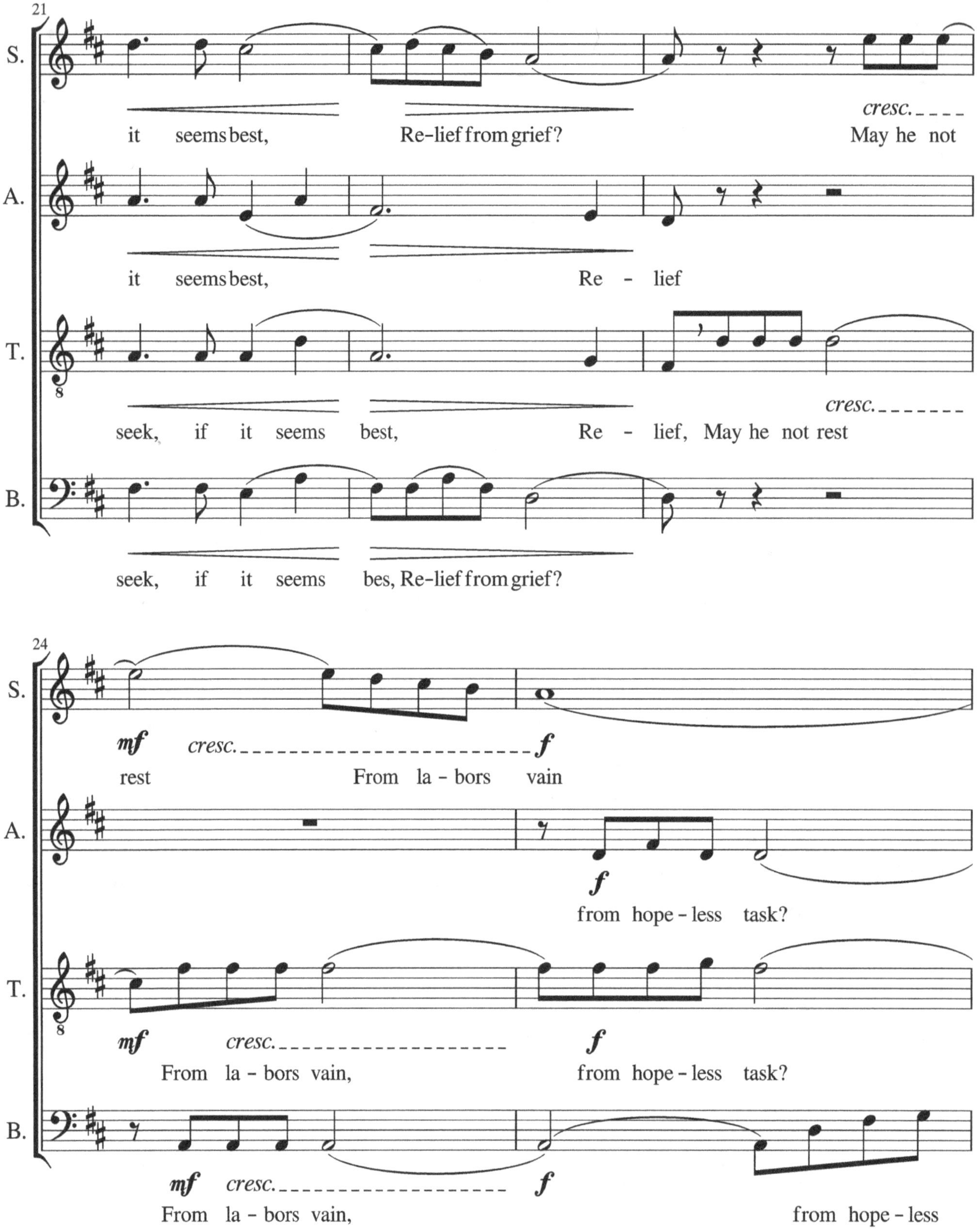

S. it seems best, Re-lief from grief? May he not

A. it seems best, Re - lief

T. seek, if it seems best, Re - lief, May he not rest

B. seek, if it seems bes, Re-lief from grief?

mf *cresc.* _ _ _ _ _ _ _ _ _ _ _ _ _ _ _ _ _ _ _ *f*

S. rest From la - bors vain

A. from hope - less task?

T. From la - bors vain, from hope - less task?

B. From la - bors vain, from hope - less

26
S.
dim.
mp
p
May he not rest from la - bors vain, from hope - less task? I do not
A.
dim.
mp
p
May he not rest From la - bors vain, from task? I do not
T.
dim.
mp
p
May he not rest From la - bors vain, from task? I do not
B.
dim.
mp
p
task? May he not rest From la - bors vain, from hope - less task? I do not
29
S.
pp
know; I on - ly ask.
A.
pp
know; I on - ly ask.
T.
pp
mf
know; I mere-ly ask. Or must he car - ry on The strug-gle, till it's
B.
pp
know; I on - ly ask.

33
S.
mf
cresc.
Or must he car-ry on The strug-gle, till it's done? The strug-gle,
A.
mf
cresc.
Or must he car-ry on The strug-gle, till it's done, The strug-gle,
T.
f
mf
cresc.
The strug-gle,
B.
mf
cresc.
Must he car - ry
36
S.
f
mp
the strug-gle, till it's done? Will he be damned, if
A.
f
mp
the strug-gle till it's done? Will he be damned, if
T.
f
mp
the strug-gle, till it's done? Will he be damned, if
B.
f
mp
on The strug - gle, till it's done? Will he be damned, if

he, World-wear-y, tired and ill, De-prived of strength and will,

he, World-wear-y, tired and ill, De-prived of strength and will,

he, World - wear - y, tired and ill,

he, World - wear - y, tired and ill,

mp
De - cides he must be free?

mp
De - cides he must be free?

mp
De - prived of strength and will,

mp
DSe - prived of strength and will,

44
S.
A.
T.
B.
cresc.
Is pun - ish - ment a - wait - ing
mp
De - cides he must be free?
cresc.
Is pun - ish - ment a - wait - ing
mp
De - cides he must be free?
46
mf
cresc.
f
those Who quit be-fore the whis-tle
mf
cresc.
f
Pun-ish-ment a - wait-ing those who quit be - fore the whis-tle
mf
cresc.
f
those Who quit be-fore the whis-tle
mf
cresc.
f
Pun-ish-ment a - wait-ing those Who quit be - fore the whis-tle

Copyright 2019 by S. T. Joshi

Lyrics under the staves:

S. (m. 49): blows, Who leave be - hind un - fin - ished task?

A. (m. 49): blows, Who leave be - hind un - fin - ished task?

T. (m. 49): blows, Who leave be - hind un - fin - ishewd task?

B. (m. 49): blows, Who leave be - hind un - fin - ished task, un - fin - ished

S. (m. 51): un - fin - ished task? Who quit be - fore the

A. (m. 51): un - fin - ished task? Who quit be - fore the

T. (m. 51): un - fin - ished task, un - fin - ished task? Who quit be - fore the

B. (m. 51): task, un - fin - ished task? Who quit be - fore the

Measure 53:

S., A., T., B.: whis-tle blows, Who leave be-hind un-fin-ished task? I do not know;

cresc. ___ *f* *p*

Measure 56:

molto rit.

S.: I on - ly ask.

A.: I mere - ly ask.

T.: I mere - ly ask.

B.: I mere - ly ask.

pp

Background

H. P. Lovecraft

S. T. Joshi

Soprano: I nev-er can be tied to raw, new things, For I first saw the light

Alto: I nev-er can be tied to raw, new things, For I first saw the light

Tenor: I nev-er can be tied to raw, new things, For I first saw the light

Bass: I nev-er can be tied to raw, new things, For I first saw the light

S.: in an old town, in an old town,

A.: in an old town, in an old

T.: in an old town, in an old town,

B.: in an old town, in an old town, in an old

S.
in an old town,

A.
town, in an old town,

T.
in an old town, Where from my win-dow huddled roofs sloped down

B.
town, in an old town,

S.
hud – dled roofs sloped down

A.
hud – dled roofs sloped down To a quaint har – bour rich with

T.
hud – dled roofs sloped down

B.
To a quaint har – bour rich with

S.
mf
rich with vi - sion-ings, rich with vi-sion-ings, with vi - sion - ings.
f

A.
mf
vi - sion-ings, with vi - sion - ings, with vi-sion-ings, with vi - sion - ings.
f

T.
mf
rich with vi - sion-ings, rich with vi-sion-ings, with vi - sion - ings.
f

B.
mf
vi - sion-ings, with vi - sion - ings, with vi-sion-ings, with vi - sion - ings.
f

S.
mp *cresc.*
Streets with carved door - ways where the sun - set beams

A.
mp *cresc.*
Streets with carved door - ways where the sun - set beams

T.
mp *cresc.*
Streets with carved door - ways where the sun - set beams

B.
mp *cresc.*
Streets with carved door - ways where the sun - set beams

20
S.
mf
cresc.
Flood - ed old fan - lights and small win - dow -
A.
mf
cresc.
old fan - lights and
T.
mf
cresc.
Flood - ed old fan - lights and small win - dow -
B.
mf
cresc.
old fan - lights and
22
S.
f
dim.
mp
panes, And Geor-gian stee-ples topped with gil-ded vanes:
A.
f
dim.
mp
small win - dow-panes, And Geor-gian stee-ples topped with gil-ded vanes:
T.
f
dim.
mp
panes And Geor-gian stee-ples topped with gil-ded vanes:
B.
f
dim.
mp
mf
small win - dow-panes, And Geor-gian stee-ples topped with gil-ded vanes: And

Copyright 2019 by S. T. Joshi

25
S.
A.
T.
mf
And Geor - gian stee - ples topped with
B.
Geor - gian stee - ples topped with gil - ded vanes, Geor - gian stee - ples topped with
27
S.
mf
And Geor - gian stee - ples topped with gil - ded
A.
mf
And Geor - gian stee - ples topped with gil - ded
T.
mp
gil - ded vanes, gil - ded vanes:
B.
mp
gil - ded vanes, gil - ded vanes:

29
S.
mp mf p
vanes, gil-ded vanes, gil-ded vanes: These were the sights that
A.
mp mf p
vanes, gil-ded vanes, gil-ded vanes: These were the sights that
T.
mp mf
gil-ded vanes:
B.
mp mf
gil-ded vanes:
32
S.
shaped my child-hood dreams.
A.
shaped my child-hood dreams.
T.
p
These were the sights that shaped my child-hood
B.
p
These were the sights that shaped my child-hood

 Copyright 2019 by S. T. Joshi

97   7

flim – sier wraiths That flit with shift – ing ways and mud – dled

flim – sier wraiths That flit with shift – ing ways and mud – dled

flim – sier wraiths That flit with shift – ing ways and mud – dled

flim – sier wraiths That flit with shif – ting ways and mud – dled

cresc. _ _ _ _ _ _ _ _ _ _ _ _ *f* *mf*

faiths A-cross the change-less walls of earth and heav'n, That flit with shift

cresc. _ _ _ _ _ _ _ _ _ _ _ _ *f* *mf*

faiths A-cross the change-less walls of earth and heav'n, That flit with shift

cresc. _ _ _ _ _ _ _ _ _ _ _ _ *f* *mf*

faiths A-cross the change-less walls of earth and heav'n, That flit with

cresc. _ _ _ _ _ _ _ _ _ _ _ _ *f* *mf*

faiths A-cross the change-less walls of earth and heav'n, That flit with

44
S.
cresc.
ing ways and mud-dled faiths A - cross the change-less walls
A.
cresc.
ing ways and mud-dled faiths A - cross the change-less walls
T.
cresc.
shift - ing ways and mud-dled faiths A - cross the change-less walls
B.
cresc.
shift - ing ways and mud-dled faiths A - cross the change-less walls
46
S.
f
of earth and heav'n.
A.
f
mp
of earth and heav'n. They cut the mo-ment's thongs and leave me
T.
f
mp
of earth and heav'n. They cut the mo-ment's thongs and leave me
B.
f
of earth and heav'n.

Copyright 2019 by S. T. Joshi

Meno mosso ♩ = **70**

S. They cut the mo-ment's thongs and leave me free
dim. *mp*

A. They cut the mo-ment's thongs and leave me free
dim. *mp*

T. They cut the mo-ment's thongs and leave me free To stand a - lone be-fore e -
dim. *mp* *f*

B. They cut the mo-ment's thongs and leave me free To stand a - lone be-fore e -
dim. *mp* *f*

S. To stand a - lone be-fore e - ter - ni-ty. To stand a - lone be-fore e -
f

A. To stand a - lone be-fore e - ter-ni - ty. To stand a - lone be-fore e -
f

T. ter - ni-ty. To stand a - lone be-fore e -

B. ter - ni-ty. To stand a - lone be-fore e -

66
S.
cresc.
ff
ter - ni-ty, e - ter - ni - ty, e - ter - ni - ty.
A.
cresc.
ff
ter - ni-ty, e - ter - ni - ty, e - ter - ni ty.
T.
cresc.
ff
ter - ni-ty, e - ter - ni - ty, e - ter - ni ty.
B.
cresc.
ff
ter - ni-ty, e - ter - ni - ty, e - ter - ni - ty.

Requiescat

Clark Ashton Smith

S. T. Joshi

Sprightly ♩ = 80

Soprano

mf
What was Love's worth? Who lived with ro - ses? Love that is

Alto

mf
What was Love's worth? Who lived with ro - ses? Love that is

Tenor

mp   *mf*
What   was   Love's   worth?   ro - ses? Love that is

Bass

mp   *mf*
What   was   Love's   worth?   ro - ses? Love that is

S.

earth,   And with earth   re - po - ses!   *mp* What   was

Α.

earth,   And with earth   re - po - ses?   *mp* What   was

T.

earth,   And with earth   re - po - ses?   *mf* What was Love's won - der?

B.

earth,   And with earth   re - po - ses?   *mf* What was Love's won - der?

7
S.
mf
Love's won - der? Af - ter the thun - der, Thun-der and show - ers!
A.
mf
Love's won - der? Af - ter the thun - der, Thun-der and show - ers!
T.
Scent of the flow - ers Af - ter the thun - der, Thun-der and show - ers!
B.
Scent of the flow - ers Af - ter the thun - der, Thun-der and show - ers!

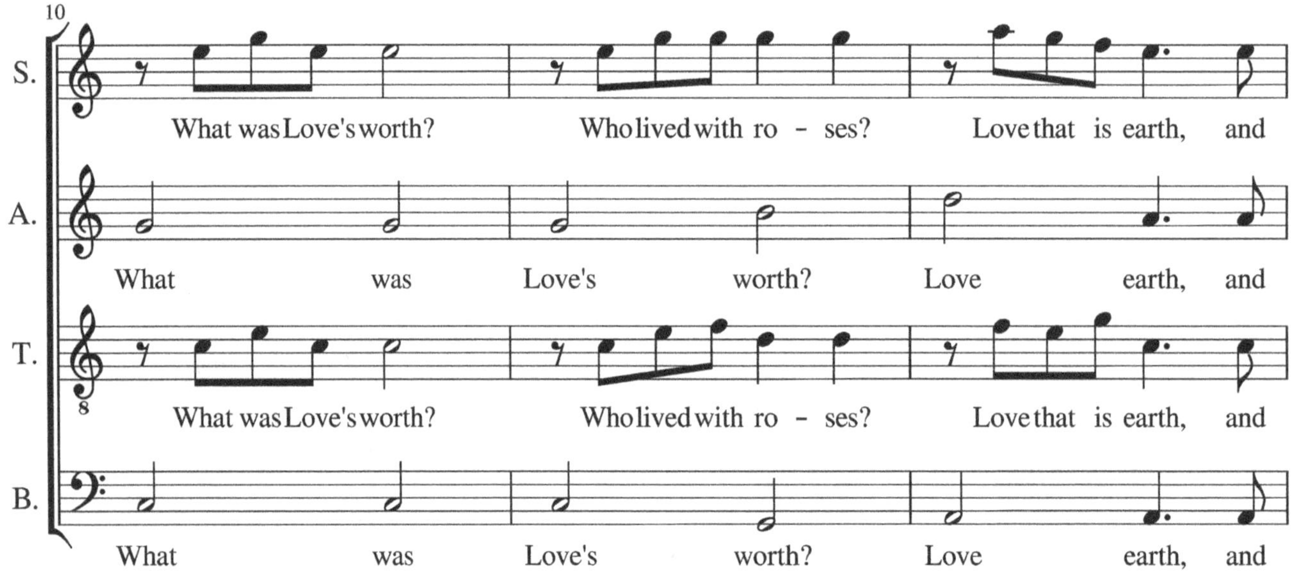
10
S.
What was Love's worth? Who lived with ro - ses? Love that is earth, and
A.
What was Love's worth? Love earth, and
T.
What was Love's worth? Who lived with ro - ses? Love that is earth, and
B.
What was Love's worth? Love earth, and

S. with earth re - po - ses! What was Love's won - der?

A. with earth re - po - ses? What was Love's won - der? Scent of the flow - ers

T. with earth re - po - ses? What was Love's won - der?

B. with earth re - po - ses? What was Love's won - der? Scent of the flow - ers

S. *mp* Af - ter the thun - der, Thun - der and show - ers! *f* What was Love's worth?

A. *mp* Af - ter the thun - der, Thun - der and show - ers! *f* What was Love's worth?

T. *mp* Af - ter the thun - der, Thun der and show - ers! *f* What was Love's worth?

B. *mp* Af - ter the thun - der, Thun - der and show - ers! *f* What was Love's worth?

Who lived with ro - ses? Love that is earth, And with earth re-po-

Who lived with ro - ses? Love that is earth, And with earth re-po-

Who lived with ro - ses? Love that is earth, And with earth re-po-

Who lived with ro - ses? Love that is earth, And with earth re-po-

ses? What was Love's won - der? Scent of the flow - ers Af - ter the thun -

ses? What was Love's won - der? Scent of the flow - ers Af - ter the thun -

ses? What was Love's won - der? Scent of the flow - ers Af - ter the thun -

ses? What was Loves won - der, Scent of the flow - ers Af - ter the thun -

der, Thun - der and show - ers, thun - der and show - ers! What were the

der, Thun - der and show - ers, thun - der and show - ers! What were the

der, Thun - der and show - ers, thun - der and show - ers! What were

der, Thun - der and show - ers, thun - der and show - ers! What were

breath - less Words that he said? Love that was death - less, Love

breath - less Words that he said? Love that was death - less, Love

the words he said? Love that was death less, Love

the words he said? Love that was death less, And with Love

Copyright 2019 by S. T. Joshi

Love that was death-less, Love that is dead! Ech - o (S.)

Love death-less, Love that is dead! Ech-o hath ta-ken (A.)

Love that was death-less, Love that is dead! Ech - o (T.)

Love death-less, Love that is dead! Ech-o hath ta-ken (B.)

hath ta - ken None shall a - wa - ken Mu-sic and moan. What (S.)

The song and flown; None shall a - wa - ken Mu-sic and moan. What (A.)

hath ta - ken None shall a - wa - ken Mu-sic and moan. What (T.)

The song and flown; None shall a - wa - ken Mu-sic and moan. What (B.)

were the breath-less Words that he said? Love that was death - less,

cresc.

were the breath-less Words that he said? Love that was death - less,

cresc.

were the breath-less Words that he said? Love that was death - less,

cresc.

were the breath-less Words that he said? Love that was death - less,

cresc.

Love that is dead! Ech-o hath ta - ken The song and flown; None

f *p*

Love with that is dead! Ech-o hath ta - ken The song and flown; None

f *p*

Love with that is dead! - Ech-o hath ta - ken The song and flown; None

f *p*

Love with that is dead! Ech-o hath ta - ken The song and flown; None

f *p*

S. shall a-wa - ken Mu - sic and moan, mu - sic and moan. Buds and the

A. shall a-wa - ken Mu - sic and moan, mu - sic and moan. Buds and the

T. shall a-wa - ken Mu - sic and moan, mu - sic and moan. Buds and the

B. shall a-wa - ken Mu - sic and moan, mu - sic and moan. Buds and the

S. flow - er, All that Love found, Last but an ho - ur, Strewn on the ground,

A. flow - er, All that Love found, Last but an ho - ur, Strewn on the ground,

T. flow - er, All that Love found, Last but an ho - ur, Stewn on the ground,

B. flow - er All that Love found, Last but an ho - ur, Strewn on the ground,

S.

*cresc.*_____   *f*   *mp*   >   *pp*

strewn on the ground, strewn on the ground, strewn on the ground.

A.

*cresc.*_____   *f*   *mp*   >   *pp*

strewn on the ground, strewn on the ground, strewn on the ground.

T.

*cresc.*_____   *f*   *mp*   >   *pp*

strewn on the ground, strewn on the ground, strewn on the ground.

B.

*cresc.*_____   *f*   *mp*   >   *pp*

strewn on the ground, strewn on the ground, strewn on the ground.

To Science

George Sterling

S. T. Joshi

Soprano: And if thou slay Him, shall the ghost not rise, not

Alto: And if thou slay Him, shall the ghost not rise, not rise, not

Tenor: And if thou slay Him, shall the ghost not rise, not rise, not

Bass: And if thou slay Him, shall the ghost not rise, not rise, not

S.: rise? Yea! if thou con-quer Him thine e - ne-my, His spec - ter from the

A.: rise? Yea! if thou con-quer Him thine e - ne-my, His spec - ter from the

T.: rise? Yea! if thou con-quer Him thine e - ne-my, His spec - ter from the

B.: rise? Yea! if thou con-quer Him thine e - ne-my, His spec - ter from the

7
S.
dim.
mf
dark shall vi - sit thee, In - vin - ci - ble, ne - ces - si - tous and wise, In - vin - ci -
A.
dim.
mf
dark shall vi - sit thee, In - vin - - - wise, In - vin - ci -
T.
dim.
mf
dark shall vi - sit thee, In - vin wise, In - vin - ci -
B.
dim.
mf
dark shall vi - sit thee, In - vin - - - wise, In - vin - ci -
10
S.
ble, ne - ces - si - tous and wise, and wise.
A.
ble, ne - ces - si - tous and wise, and wise.
T.
ble, ne - ces - si - tous and wise, and wise. And if thou slay Him,
B.
ble, ne - ces - si - tous and wise, and wise. And if thou slay Him,

13
S.
A.
f
And if thou slay Him, shall the ghost not rise?
T.
shall the ghost not rise?
f
And if thou slay Him, shall the ghost not rise?
B.
f
shall the ghost not rise?
16
S.
mp
And if thou slay Him, shall the ghost not rise?
f
Yea! if thou
A.
f
Yea! if thou
T.
f
Yea! if thou
B.
mp
And if thou slay Him, shall the ghost not rise?
f
Yea! if thou

con-quer Him thine e - ne - my, His spec - ter from the dark shall vi - sit thee, (S.)

con-quer Him thine e - ne - my, His spec - ter from the dark shall vi - sit thee, (A.)

con-quer Him thine e - ne - my, His spec - ter from the dark shall vi - sit thee, (T.)

con-quer Him thine e - ne - my, His spec - ter from the dark shall vi - sit thee, (B.)

In - vin - ci - ble, ne - ces - si-tous and wise, and wise. (S.)

In - vin - ci-ble, ne - ces - si-tous and wise. and wise. (A.)

In - vin - ci - ble, and wise. and wise. (T.)

In - vin - ci - ble, and and wise. and wise, (B.)

The ty-rant and mi-rage of hu-man eyes, of hu-man eyes, Ex-
The ty-rant and mi-rage of hu-man eyes, of hu-man eyes, Ex-
The ty-rant and mi-rage of hu-man eyes, of hu-man eyes, Ex-
The ty-rant and mi-rage of hu-man eyes, of hu-man eyes, Ex-

haled up-on the spir-it's dark-ened sea, Shares He thy mo-ment of e-
haled up-on the spir-it's dark-ened sea, Shares He thy mo-ment of e-
haled up-on the spir-it's dark-ened sea, Shares He thy mo-ment of e-
haled up-on the spir-it's dark-ened sea, Shares He thy mo-ment of e-

System S. / A. / T. / B. measure 31:

ter - ni-ty,   Thy truth con - front-ed ev - er with his (S.)

ter - ni-ty,   e - ter - ni-ty, Thy truth con - front-ed ev - er   with his (A.)

ter - ni-ty, e - ter - ni-ty,   e - ter - ni-ty, Thy truth con - front-ed ev - er with his (T.)

ter - ni-ty,   e - ter - ni-ty, Thy truth con - front-ed ev - er with his (B.)

System measure 34:

lies. (S.)

lies. (A.)

lies.   *mf* Ex-haled up - on the spir - it's (T.)

lies. The ty-rant and mi-rage of hu - man eyes, (B.)   *mf*

S. Thy truth con-front-ed ev - er

A. Shares He thy mo - ment of e - ter - ni-ty, Thy truth con-front-ed ev - er

T. dark-ened sea, Thy truth con-front-ed ev - er

B. Thy truth con-front-ed ev - er

S. with His lies, His lies. Thy ban - ners gleam a lit-tle and are furled;

A. with His lies, His lies. Thy ban - ners gleam a lit-tle and are furled;

T. with His lies, His lies. Thy ban - ners gleam a lit-tle and are furled;

B. with His lies, His lies. Thy ban - ners gleam a lit-tle and are furled;

Against thy turrets surge His phantom tow'rs; Drugged with His opiates the nations nod, Refusing still the beauty

48
S.
mf
of thine hours; A-
A.
of thine hours;
T.
mf
cresc.
f
of thine hours; Thy ban-ners gleam a lit-tle, a lit-tle and are furled;
B.
of thine hours;
51
S.
gainst thy tur - rets surge His phan-tom tow'rs;
A.
mf
Drugged with His o - pi-ates the na-tions
T.
B.

S. Re-fu-sing still the beau-ty of thine hours, the beau-ty of thine

A. nod, Re-fu-sing still the beau-ty of thine hours, the beau-ty of thine

T. Re-fu-sing still the beau-ty of thine hours, the beau-ty of thine

B. Re-fu-sing still the beau-ty of thine hours, the beau-ty of thine

S. hours, the beau-ty of thine hours; And frag-ile is thy ten-ure of this

A. hours, the beau-ty of thine hours; And frag-ile is thy ten-ure of this

T. hours, the beau-ty of thine hours; And frag-ile is thy ten-ure of this

B. hours, the beau-ty of thine hours; And frag-ile is thy ten-ure of this

61
S.
world
And frag - ile is thy ten-ure of this world Still
A.
world, this world
frag - ile is thy ten-ure of this world, Still
T.
world, thus world
frag - ile is thy ten-ure of this world Still
B.
world, this world, frag - ile is thy ten-ure of this world Still
64
S.
cresc.
mf
haunt-ed by the mon strous ghost of God, the mon - strous ghost of
A.
mf
haunt-ed by the mon strous ghost of God, the mon - strous ghost of
T.
mf
haunt-ed by the mon strous ghost of God, the mon - strous ghost of
B.
mf
haunt-ed by the mon strous ghost of God, the mon - strous ghost of

S.

God, the mon - strous ghost of God.

A.

God, the mon - strous ghost of God.

T.

God, the mon - strous ghost of God.

B.

God, the mon - strous ghost of God.

Little Sam Perkins

To the Memory of Henry the Cat

H. P. Lovecraft

S. T. Joshi

Soprano: The an - cient gar - den seems to - night A deep - er gloom to

Alto: The an - cient gar - den seems to - night A deep - er gloom to

bear,

bear,

Tenor: The an - cient gar - den seems to - night A deep - er gloom to

Bass: The an - cient gar - den seems to - night A deep - er gloom to

S. The an-cient gar-den seems to-night A deep-er gloom to

A. The an-cient gar-den seems to-night A deep-er gloom to

T. bear, The an-cient gar-den seems to-night A deep-er gloom to

B. bear, The an-cient gar-den seems to-night A deep-er gloom to

S. bear, As if some si-lent shad-ow's blight Were hov-'ring in the

A. bear, As if some si-lent shad-ow's blight Were hov-'ring in the

T. bear, As if some si-lent shad-ow's

B. bear, As if some si-lent shad-ow's

9
S.
f
mp
mf
air. hov-'ring in the air, As if some
A.
f
mp
mf
air. hov-'ring in the air, As if some
T.
f
mp
mf
mf
blight Were hov-'ring in the air. As if some
B.
f
mf
mf
blight Were hov-'ring in the air. As if some
13
S.
dim.
p
mp
si - lent shad-ow's blight Were hov-'ring in the air. With hid-den griefs the
A.
dim.
p
mp
si - lent shad-ow's blight Were hov-'ring in the air. With hid-den griefs the
T.
dim.
p
mp
si - lent shad-ow's blight Were hov-'ring in the air. With hid-den griefs the
B.
p
mp
si - lent shad-ow's blight Were hov-'ring in the air. With hid-den griefs the

S. grass-es sway, Un-a-ble quite to word them,

A. grass-es sway, Un-a-ble quite to word them, Un-a-ble quite to

T. grass-ses sway, Un-a-ble quite to word

B. grass-ses sway,

S. Un-a-ble quite to word them, word them,

A. word them, Un-a-ble quite to

T. them, Un-a-ble quite to word them,

B. Un-a-ble quite to word them, word them,

22
S.
A.
T.
B.
mf
mp
p
word them, Un-a-ble quite to word them, word them, Re-mem - ber-ing from
Un-a-ble quite to word them, word them,
27
dim.
yes-ter-day The lit-tle paws that stirr'd them.
Re-mem-ber-ing from yes-ter -

30
S.
mp
Re-mem-ber - ing from yes-ter-day The
A.
mp
Re-mem-ber - ing from yes-ter-day The
T.
mp p mp
day The lit-tle paws that stirr'd them, Re-mem-ber - ing from yes-ter-day The
B.
mp p mp
day The lit-tle paws that stirr'd them, Re-mem-ber - ing from yes-ter-day The
33
S.
cresc. mf f p
lit - tle paws that stirr'd them, stirr'd them, stirr'd them, The lit-tle
A.
cresc. mf f p
lit - tle paws that stirr'd them, stirr'd them, stirr'd them, The lit-tle
T.
cresc. mf f p
lit - tle paws that stirr'd them, stirr'd them, stirr'd them, The lit-tle
B.
cresc. mf f p
lit - tle paws that stirr'd them, stirr'd them, stirr'd them, The lit-tle

37
S.
dim.
pp
paws that stirr'd them.
A.
dim.
pp
paws that stirr'd them.
T.
dim.
pp
paws that stirr'd them.
B.
dim.
pp
paws that stirr'd them.

A Dirge of Victory

Lord Dunsany

S. T. Joshi

♩ = 60

Soprano: Lift not thy trum-pet, Vic-to - ry, to the sky, Nor through bat - tal-lions

Alto: Lift not thy trum-pet, Vic-to - ry, to the sky, Nor through bat - tal-lions

Tenor: Lift not thy trum-pet, Vic-to - ry, to the sky, Nor through bat - tal-lions

Bass: Lift not thy trum - pet to the sky, Nor through bat - tal-lions

S.: nor by bat'-tries blow, Lift not thy trum-pet, Vic-to-ry,

A.: nor by bat'-tries blow, Lift not ty trum-pet, Vic-to-ry,

T.: nor by bat'-tries blow, trum-pet Vic-to-

B.: nor by bat'-tries blow, trum-pet Vic-to-

S. Nor through bat - tal - lions nor by bat'-tries blow,

A. Nor through bat - tal - lions nor by bat'-tries blow,

T. ry, Nor through bat - tal - lions nor by bat'-tries blow, But o - ver
mf

B. ry, Nor through bat - tal - lions nor by bat'-tries blow, But o - ver
mf

S. *mf*
But o - ver hol-lows full of old wire go,

A. *mf*
But o - ver hol-lows full of old wire go,

T. hol-lows full of old wire go,

B. hol-lows full of old wire go,

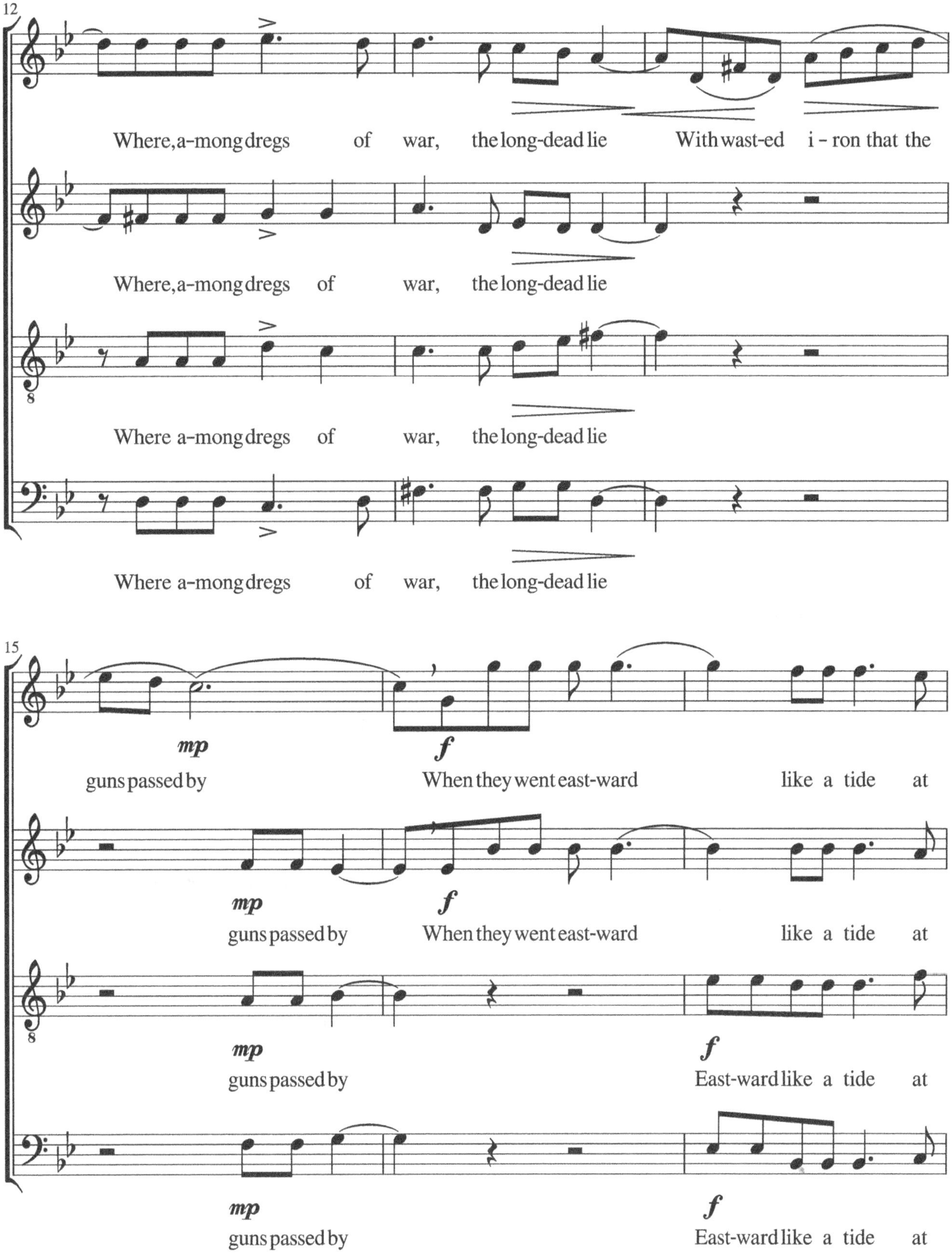

12
S.
Where, a-mong dregs of war, the long-dead lie With wast-ed i - ron that the
A.
Where, a-mong dregs of war, the long-dead lie
T.
Where a-mong dregs of war, the long-dead lie
B.
Where a-mong dregs of war, the long-dead lie
15
S.
mp
f
guns passed by When they went east-ward like a tide at
A.
mp
f
guns passed by When they went east-ward like a tide at
T.
mp
f
guns passed by East-ward like a tide at
B.
mp
f
guns passed by East-ward like a tide at

18
S.
dim.
flow; There blow thy trum - pet that the dead may know,
A.
dim.
blow; There blow thy trum - pet that the dead may know, dead may know,
T.
dim.
flow; There blow thy trum - pet that the dead may know, dead may know,
B.
dim.
flow; There blow thy trum - pet that the dead may know, dead may know,
20
S.
mf
Who wait-ed for thy com-ing, Vic-to-ry,
A.
mf
dead may know, dead may know, Who wait-ed for thy com-ing, Vic-to-ry, Vic-to-
T.
mf
dead may know, dead may know, Who wait-ed for thy com-ing, Vic-to-ry, Vic-to-
B.
mf
dead may know, dead may know, Who wait-ed for thy com-ing, Vic-to-ry, Vic-to-

Who wait-ed for thy com-ing, Vic-to-ry, Vic-to-ry. It is not we that

ry, Who wait-ed for thy com-ing, Vic-to-ry, Vic-to-ry. It is not we that

ry, Who wait-ed for thy com-ing, Vic-to-ry, Vic-to-ry. It is not we that

ry, Who wait-ed for thy com-ing, Vic-to-ry, Vic-to-ry. It is not we that

have de-served thy wreath. It is not we that have de-

have De-served thy wreath. It is not we that have de-

have De-served thy wreath. It is not we that have de-

have De-served thy wreath. It is not we that have de-

Copyright 2021 by S. T. Joshi

Lyrics (under staves):

The deep mud burned un – der the ther-mite's breath, And win-ter crack'd the

breath, The deep mud burned un – der the ther-mite's breath, And win-ter crack'd the

bones that no man needs: Hun-dreds of nights flamed by: the sea-sons passed. Hun-

Lyrics under the staves:

S. (m. 43): dreds of nights flamed by: the sea-sons passed.

A. (m. 43): dreds of nights flamed by: the sea-sons passed.

T. (m. 43): dreds of nights flamed by: the sea-sons passed. And thou hast come to them at

B. (m. 43): dreds of nights flamed by: the sea-sons passed.

S. (m. 46): And thou hast come to them at last, at last!

A. (m. 46): And thou hast come to them at last, at last!

T. (m. 46): last, at last! And thou hast come to them at last, at last, at last, at

B. (m. 46): And thou hast come to them at last, at last, at last,

49
rit.
S.
cresc.
ff
mp
pp
at last, at last; at last; at last!
A.
at last, at last, at last, at last; at last; at last!
T.
last; at last; at last; at last!
B.
at last; at last; at last!

Imprisoned

Mary K. Wilson

S. T. Joshi

Lilting ♩ = 70

Soprano

mp *cresc.___* *mf* *cresc._* *f*
You can-not climb too high; The fort-ress is made of steel, Its

Alto

mp *cresc.___* *mf* *cresc._* *f*
You can-not climb too high; The fort-ress is made of steel, Its

Tenor

mp *cresc.___* *mf* *cresc._* *f*
You can-not climb too high; The fort-ress is made of steel, Its

Bass

mp *cresc.___* *mf* *cresc._* *f*
You can-not climb too high, too high; The fort-ress is made of steel, Its

S.

dim.____ *mp*
win-dows are black and sealed, And its walls are steeped in lye.

A.

dim.____ *mp*
win-dows are black and sealed, walls are steeped in lye.

T.

dim.____ *mp*
win-dows are black and sealed, walls are steeped in lye.

B.

dim.____ *mp* *mf*
win-dows are black and sealed, are sealed, walls are steeped in lye. You

17
S.
A.
mf
Its win-dows are
T.
f
mf
The fort-ress is made of steel, Its win-dows are
B.
cresc.
f
mf
can-not climb too high; The fort-ress is made of steel, of steel, Its win-dows are
26
S.
mp
And its walls are steeped in lye. How do you e -
A.
mp
p
black and sealed, walls are steeped in lye. Ah
T.
mp
p
black and sealed, walls are steeped in lye. Ah
B.
mp
p
black and sealed, and sealed, walls are steeped in lye. Ah

Copyright 2021 by S. T. Joshi

S. merge from hell? Where is the ex-it to flee? You scream out:"Let me be free!"

cresc. *mf* *f*

A. cresc. *mf*

T. cresc. *mf*

B. cresc. *mf*

S. Ech-oes die in a dark cell. The floor is i-cy and cold;

p *mp*

A. Ech-oes die in a dark cell. The floor is i-cy and cold,

p *mp*

T. Ech-oes die in a dark cell. The floor is i-cy and cold;

p *mp*

B. Ech-oes die in a dark cell, dark cell. The floor is i-cy and cold, and cold;

p *mp*

S. (53)
Hiss-ing winds shat-ter your ears And mag-ni-fy ev'-ry fear Un-til
cresc. _____ *mf*

A.
Hiss-ing winds shat-ter your ears And mag-ni-fy ev'-ry fear
cresc. _____ *mf*

T.
Hiss-ing winds shat-ter your ears And mag-ni-fy ev'-ry fear
cresc. _____ *mf*

B.
Hiss-ing winds shat-ter your ears And mag-ni-fy ev'ry fear
cresc. _____ *mf*

S. (61)
your young soul grows old. Ah Ah
mp *p* *cresc.*

A.
your young soul grows old. Ah Ah
mp *p* *cresc.*

T.
your young soul grows old. Ah Hiss-ing winds
mp *p* *cresc.* *f*

B.
your young soul grows old. The floor is i-cy and cold; Ah
mp *mf* *cresc.*

146   Copyright 2021 by S. T. Joshi

70
S.
A.
T.
B.
mf
dim.
And mag-ni-fy ev'-ry fear Ah
mp dim.
Un - til your young soul grows old.
mp
dim.
shat-ter your ears Ah
Ah
dim.
80
mp cresc. mf cresc.
You yearn for rays of sun - light, Yet on - ly charred dust pre - vails;
mp cresc. mf cresc.
You yearn for rays of sun - light, Yet on - ly charred dust pre - vails;
mp cresc. mf cresc.
You yearn for rays of sun - light, Yet on - ly charred dust pre - vails;
mp cresc. mf cresc.
You yearn for rays of sun - light, sun - light, Yet on - ly charred dust pre - vails;

It cov-ers your face so pale; Eyes blind-ed, you die from fright, from

It cov-ers your face so pale; Eyes blind-ed, you die from fright, from

It cov-ers your face so pale; Eyes blind-ed, you die from fright, from

It cov-ers your face so pale; Eyes blind-ed, you die from fright, from

fright, from fright, from fright.

fright, from fright, from fright.

fright, from fright, from fright.

fright, from fright, from fright.

TRUMPET CONCERTO IN D

Trumpet Concerto in D
I.

S. T. Joshi

Copyright 2021 by S. T. Joshi

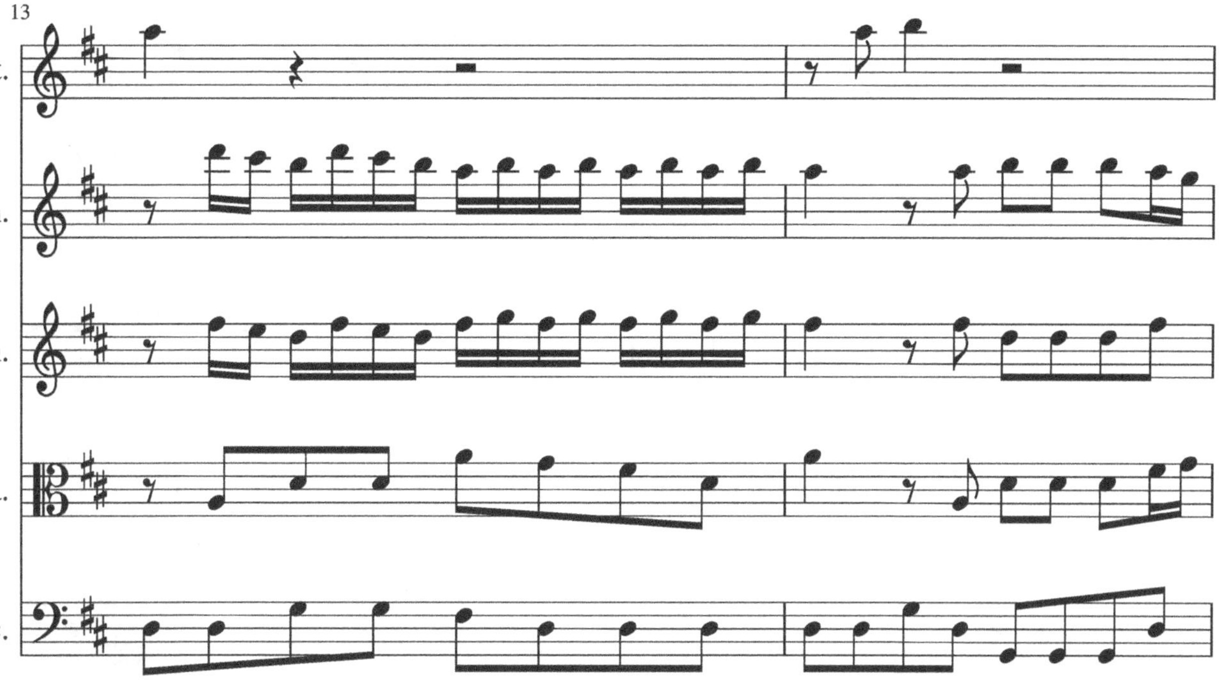
13
C Tpt.
Vln.
Vln.
Vla.
Vc.

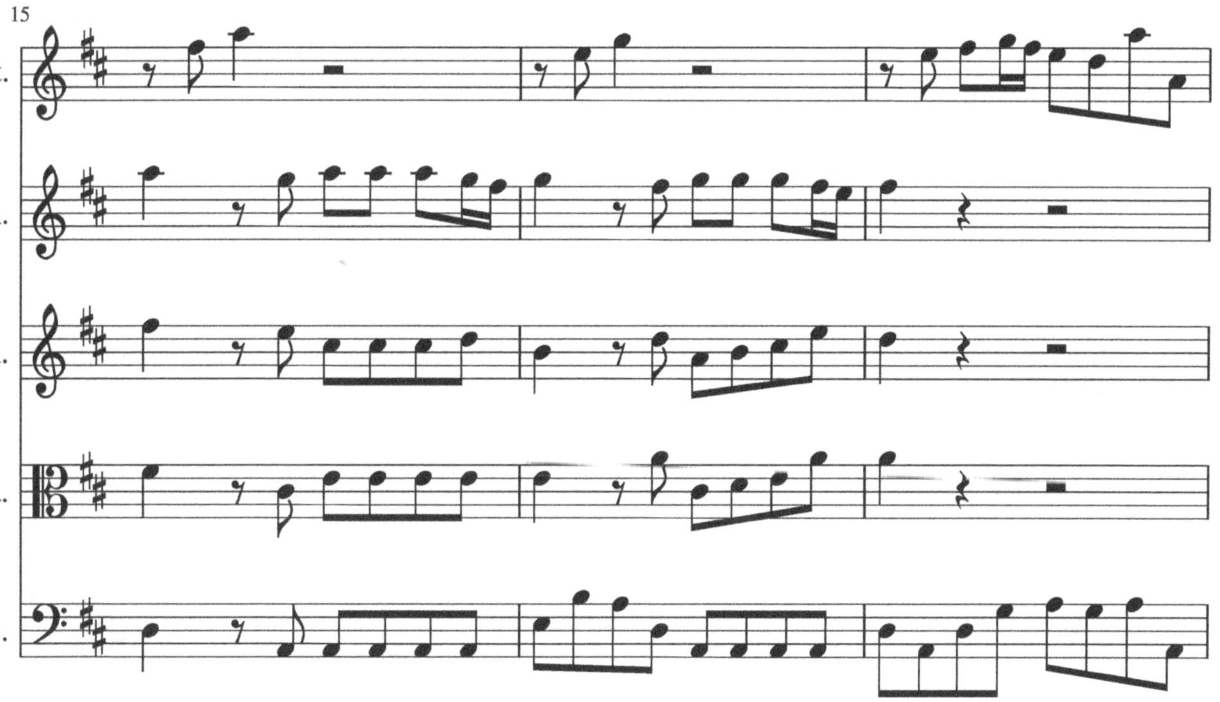
15
C Tpt.
Vln.
Vln.
Vla.
Vc.

Copyright 2021 by S. T. Joshi

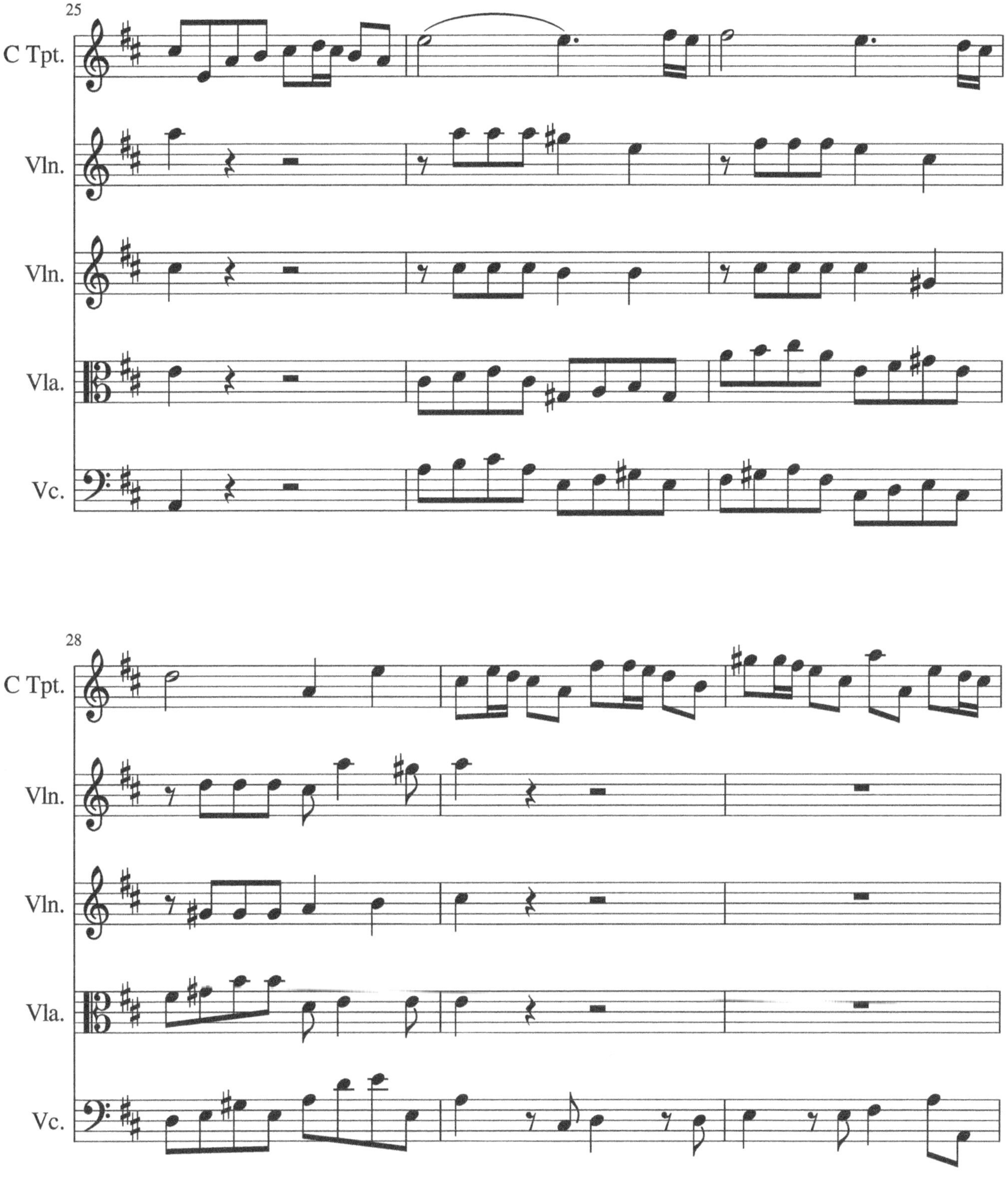
25
C Tpt.
Vln.
Vln.
Vla.
Vc.
28
C Tpt.
Vln.
Vln.
Vla.
Vc.

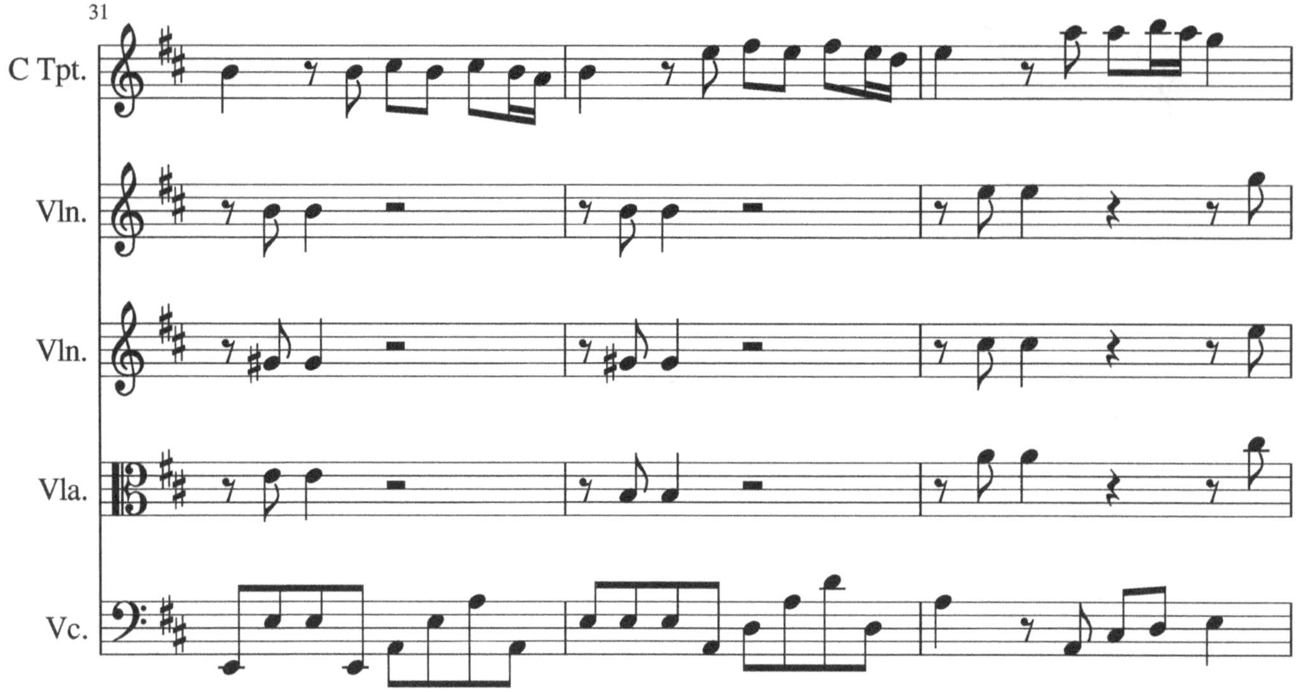
31
C Tpt.
Vln.
Vln.
Vla.
Vc.

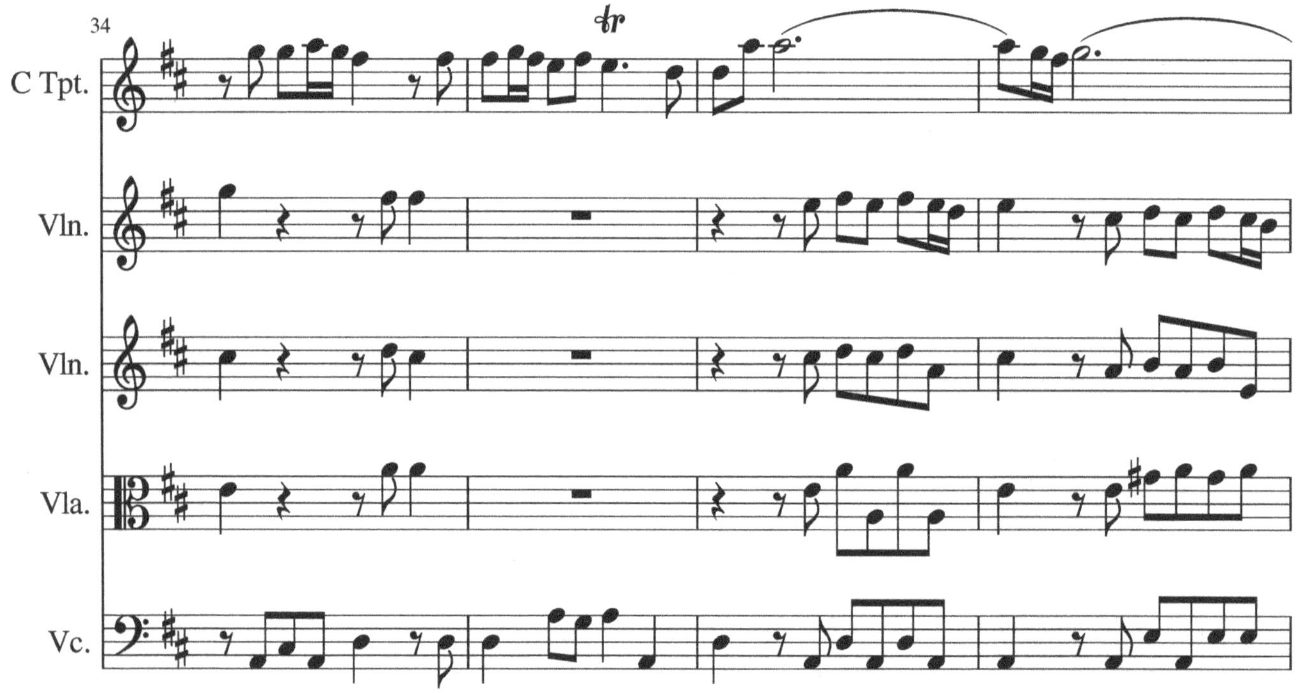
34
tr
C Tpt.
Vln.
Vln.
Vla.
Vc.

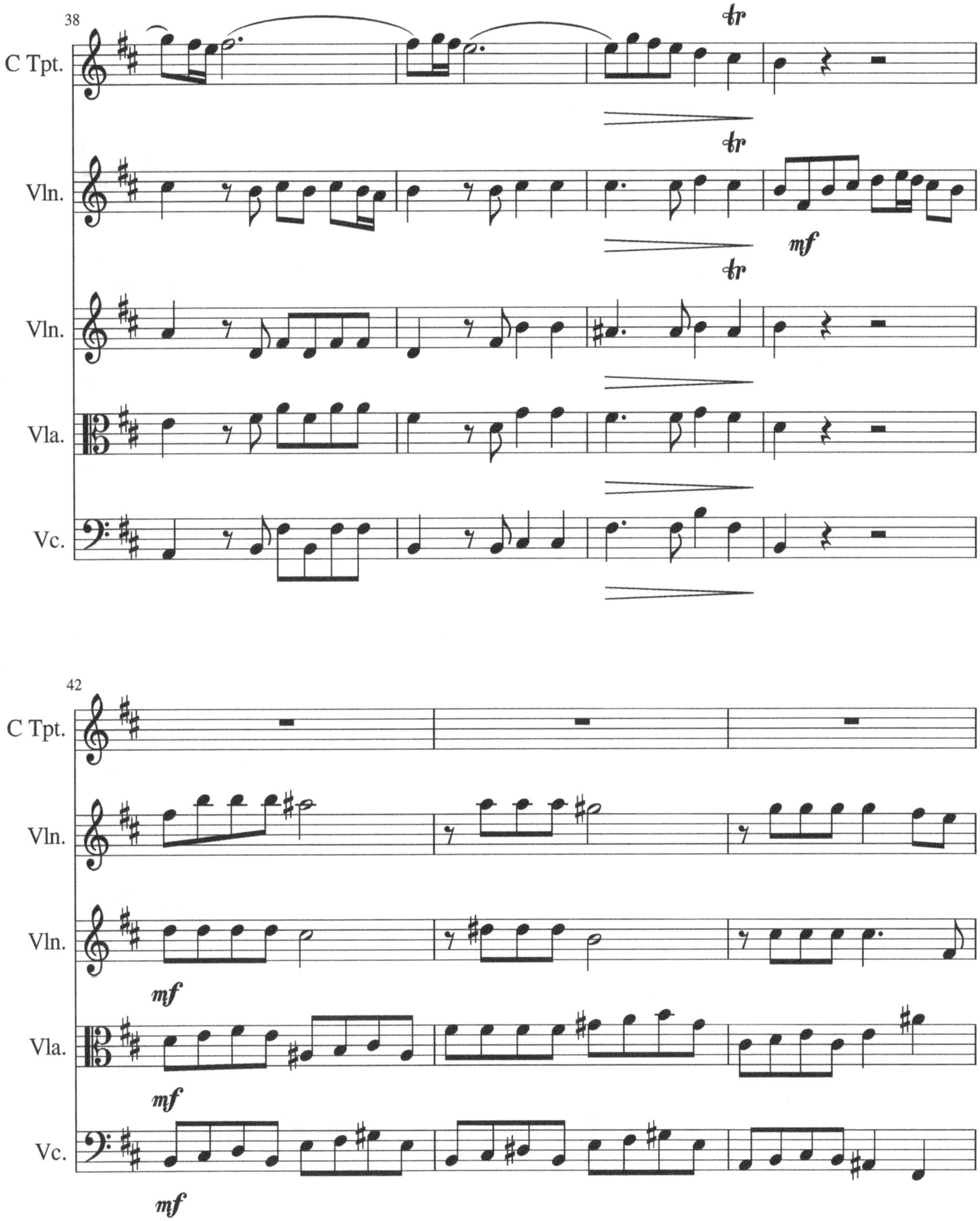
38
C Tpt.
Vln.
Vln.
Vla.
Vc.
tr
tr
tr
mf
42
C Tpt.
Vln.
Vln.
Vla.
Vc.
mf
mf
mf

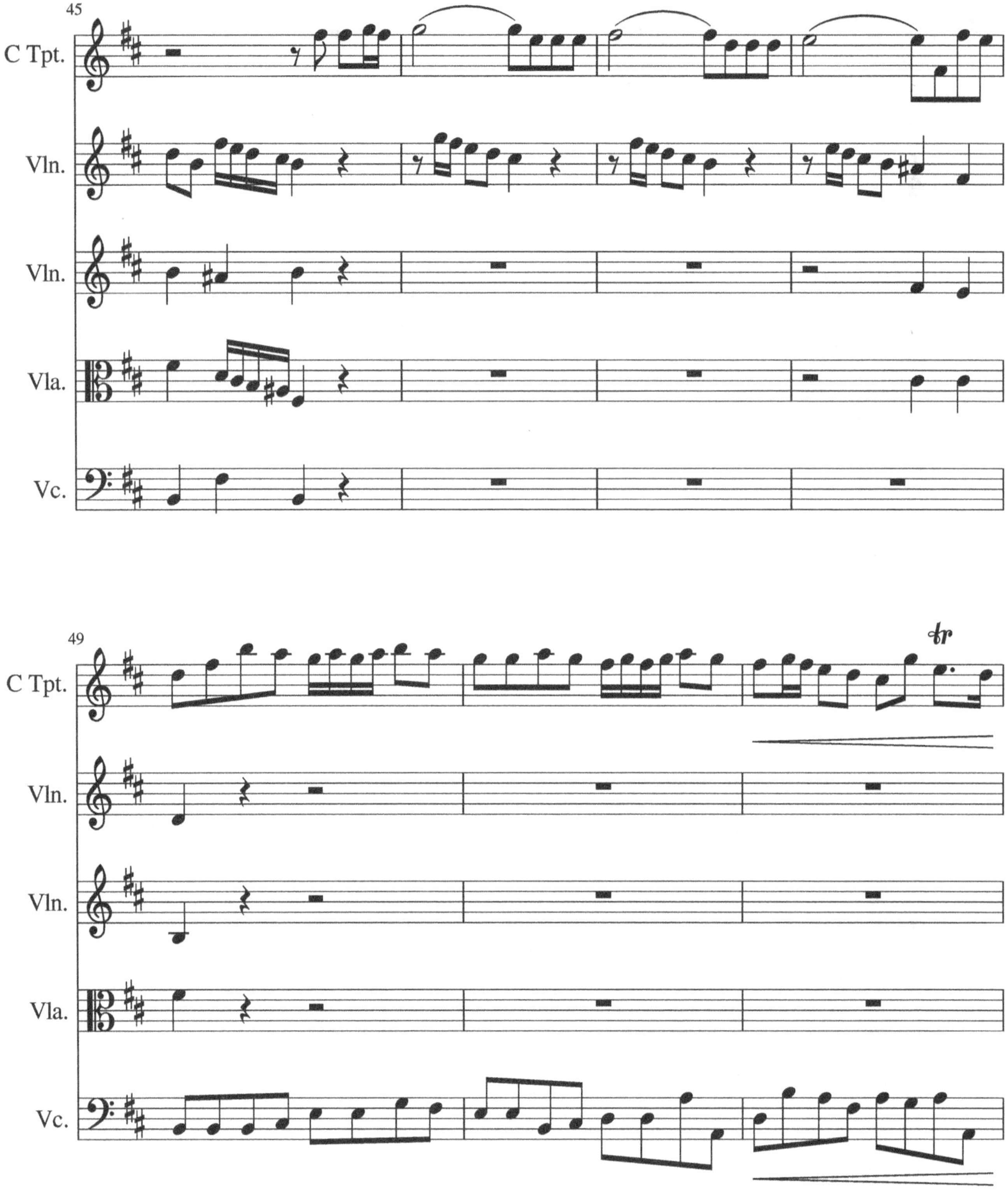
45
C Tpt.
Vln.
Vln.
Vla.
Vc.
49
C Tpt.
Vln.
Vln.
Vla.
Vc.

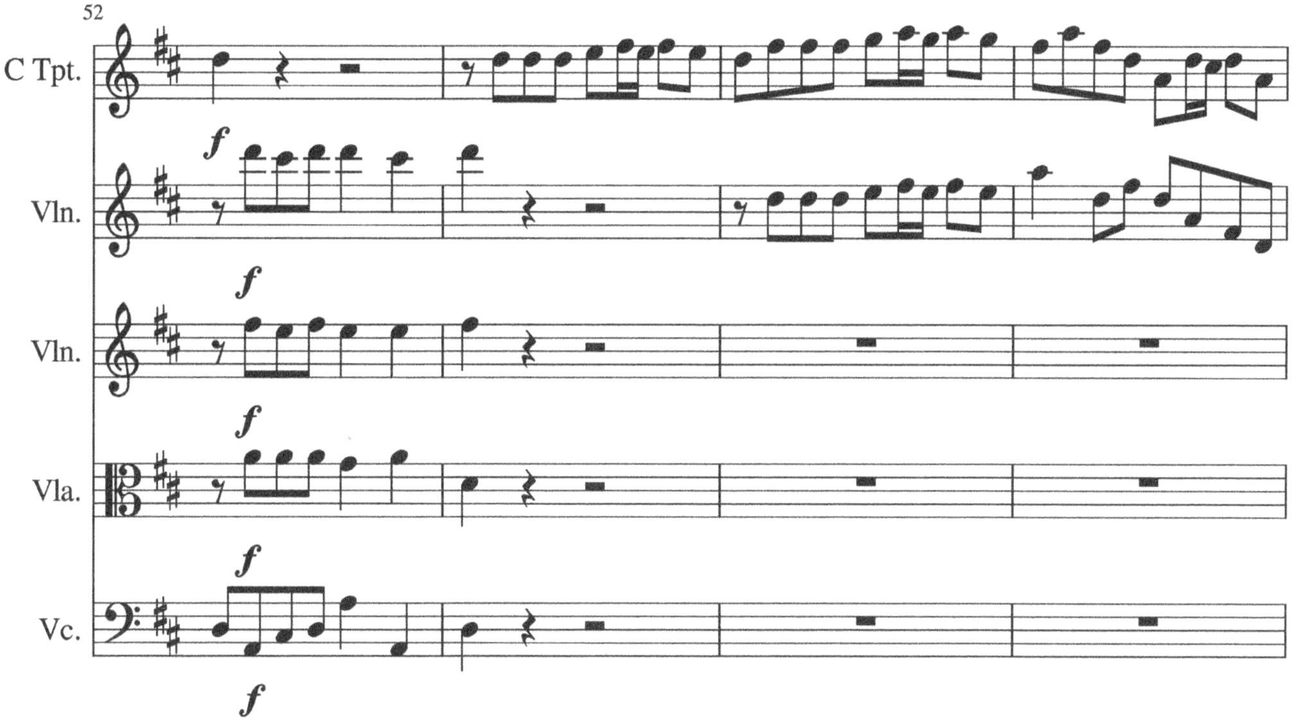
52
C Tpt.
Vln.
Vln.
Vla.
Vc.
f
f
f
f
f

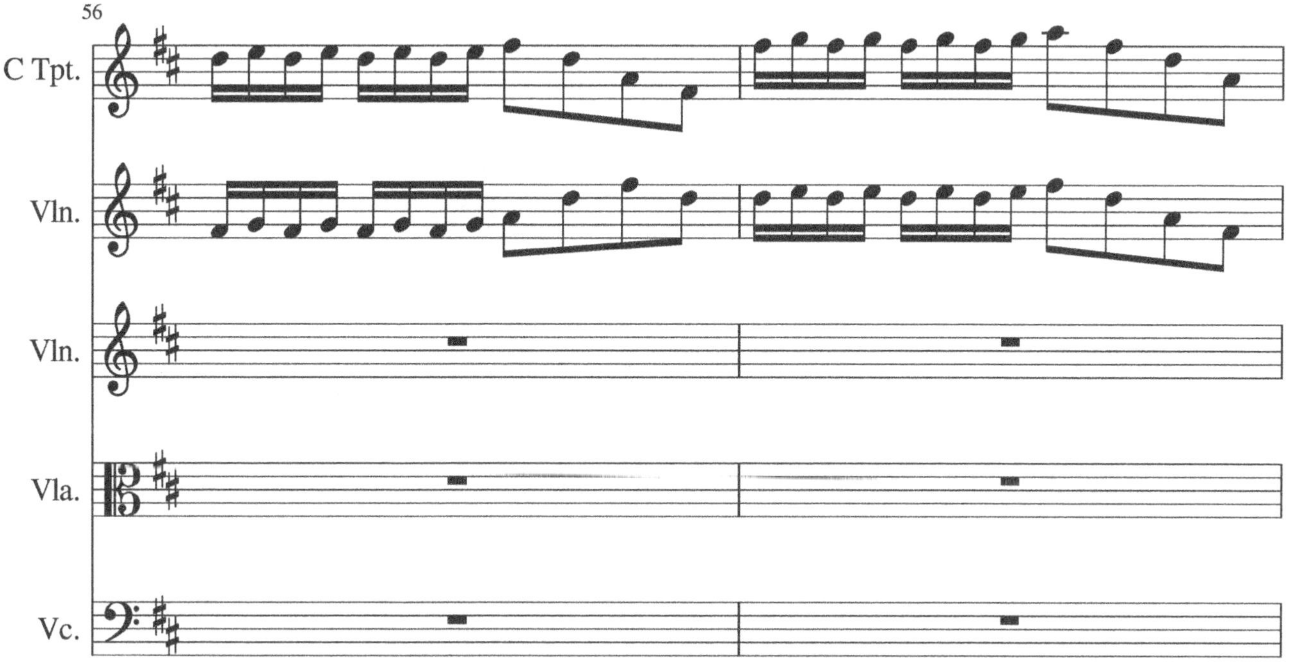
56
C Tpt.
Vln.
Vln.
Vla.
Vc.

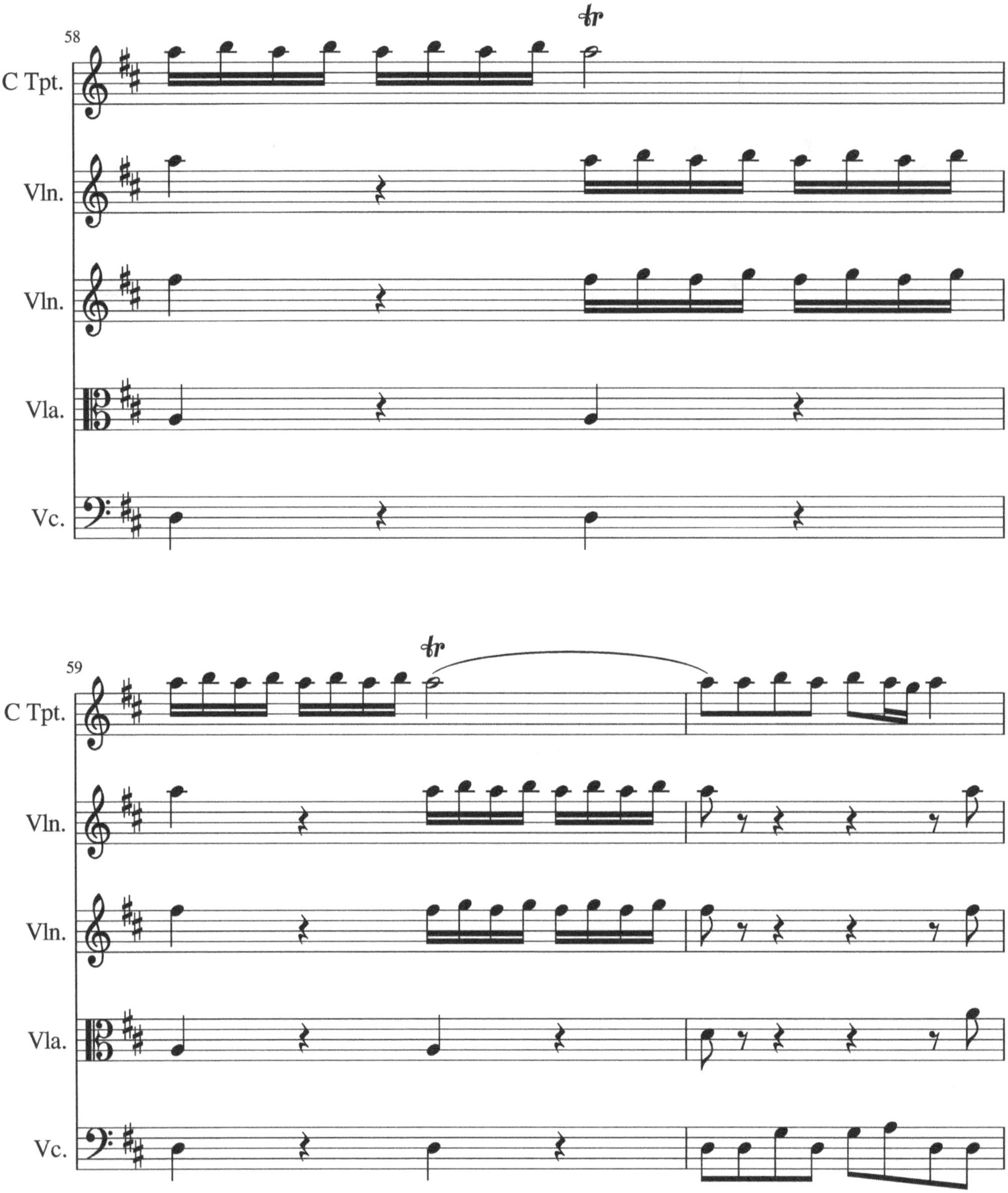

tr
58
C Tpt.
Vln.
Vln.
Vla.
Vc.
tr
59
C Tpt.
Vln.
Vln.
Vla.
Vc.

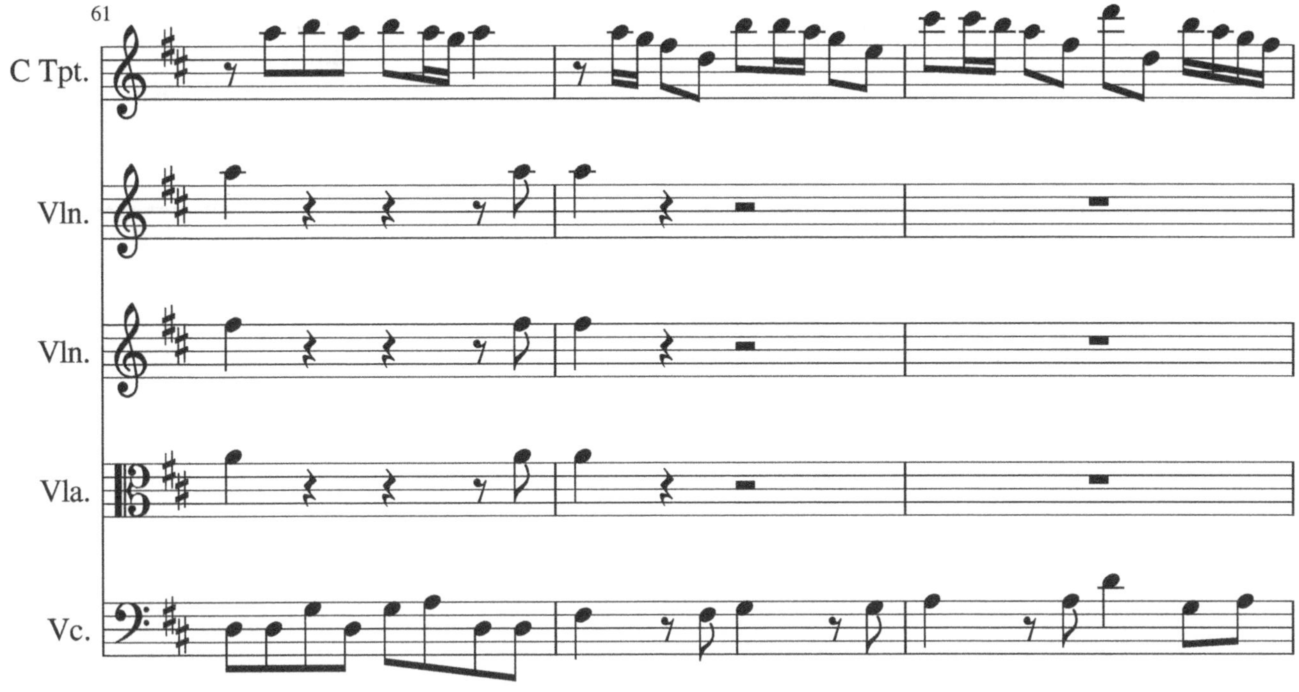
61
C Tpt.
Vln.
Vln.
Vla.
Vc.

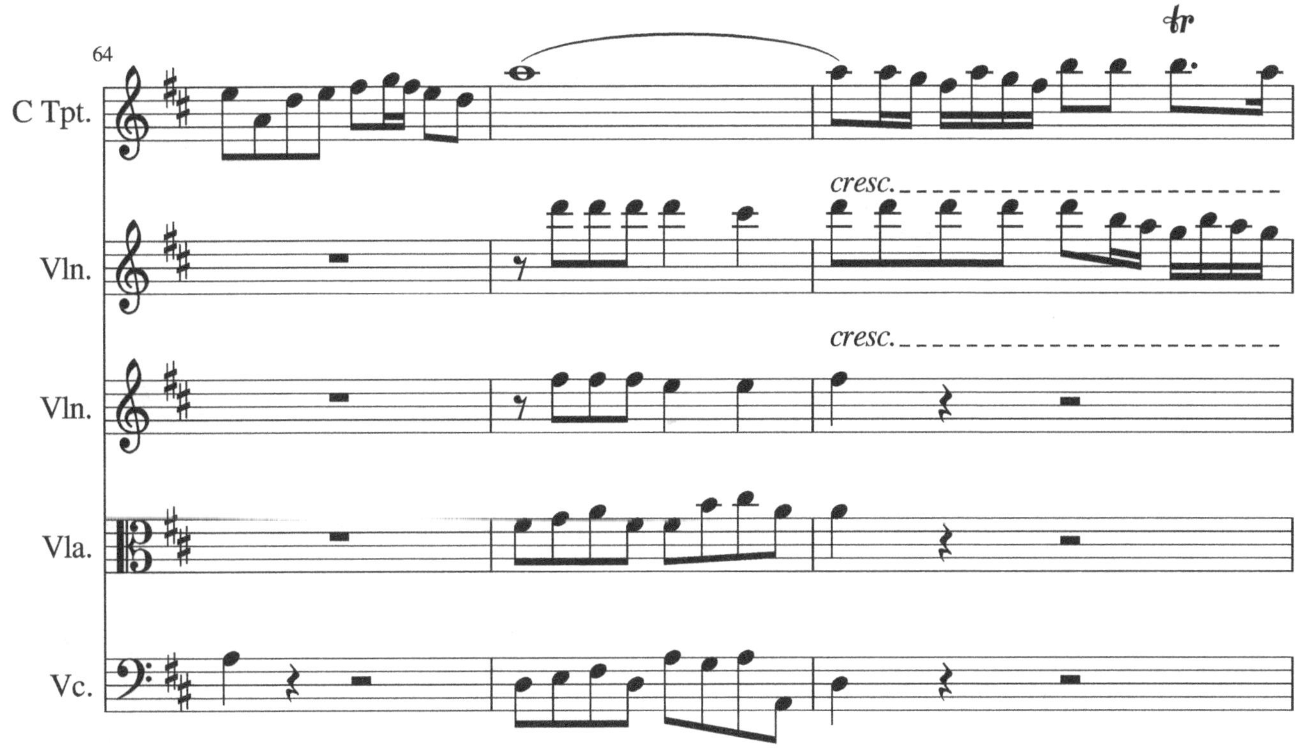
64
C Tpt.
tr
cresc.
Vln.
cresc.
Vln.
Vla.
Vc.

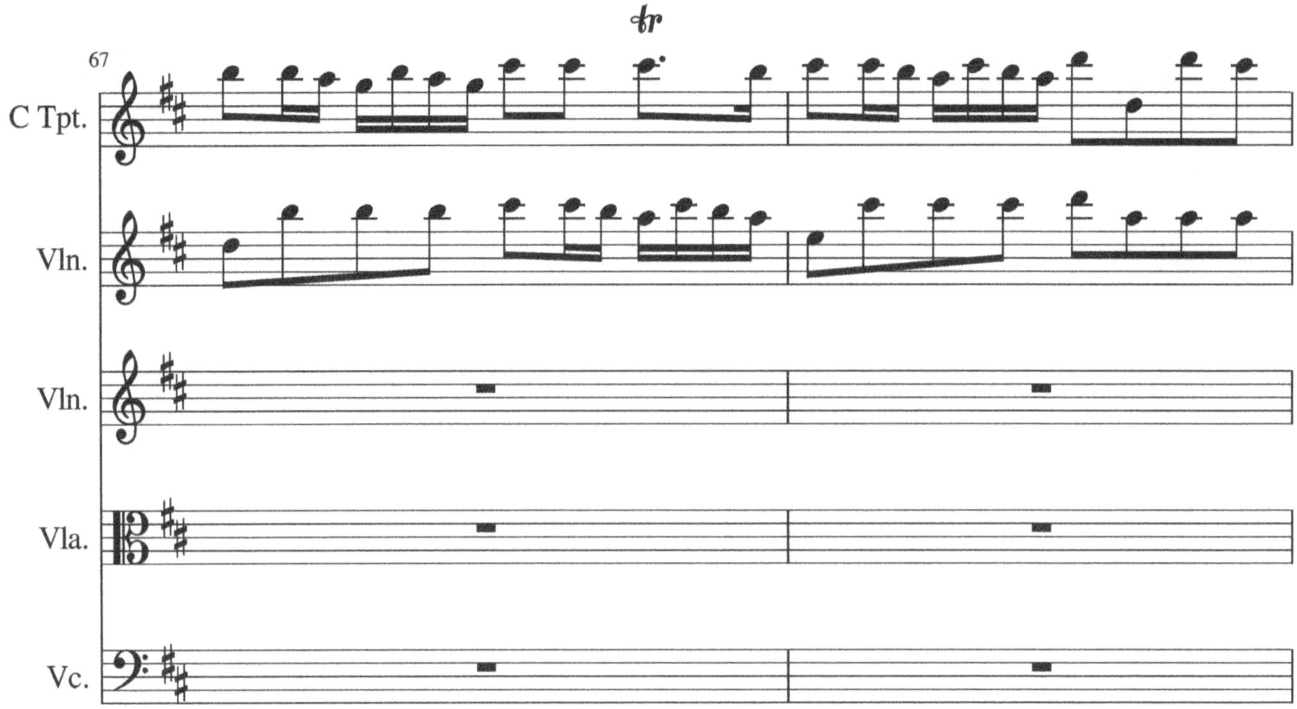
tr
67
C Tpt.
Vln.
Vln.
Vla.
Vc.

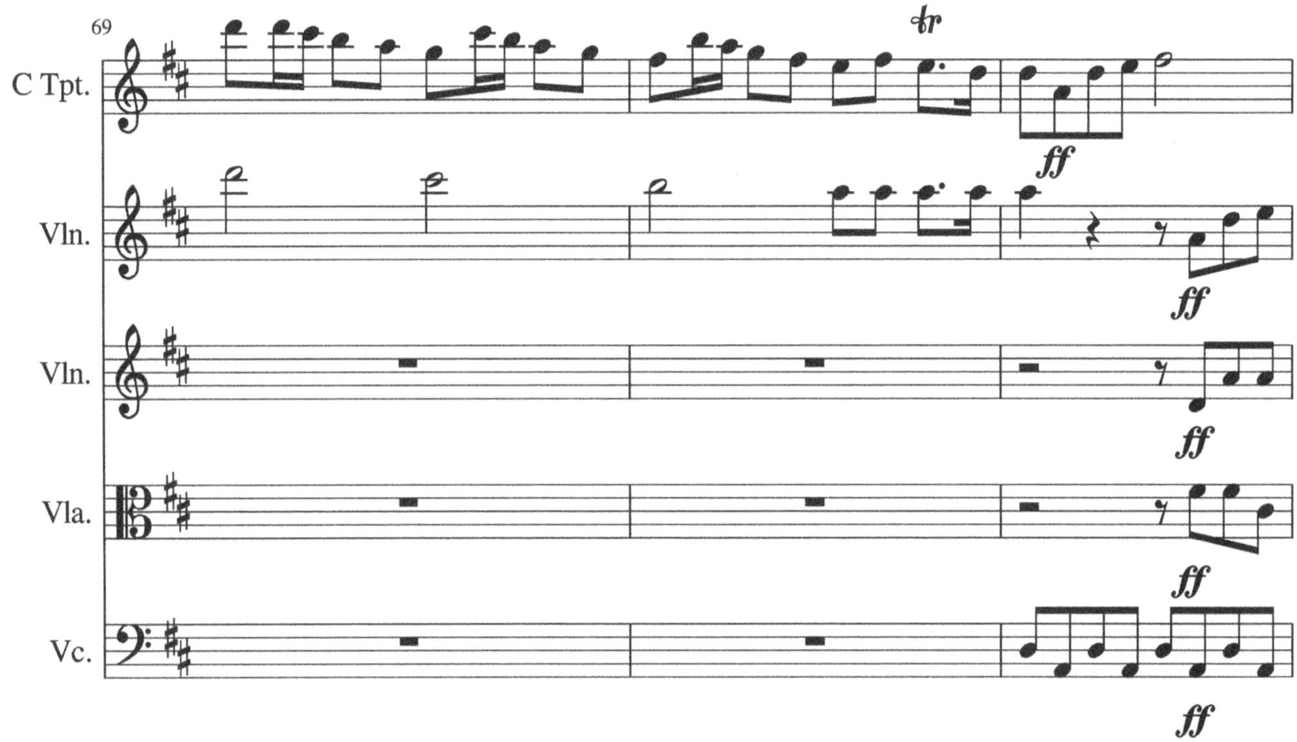
69
tr
C Tpt.
ff
Vln.
ff
Vln.
ff
Vla.
ff
Vc.
ff

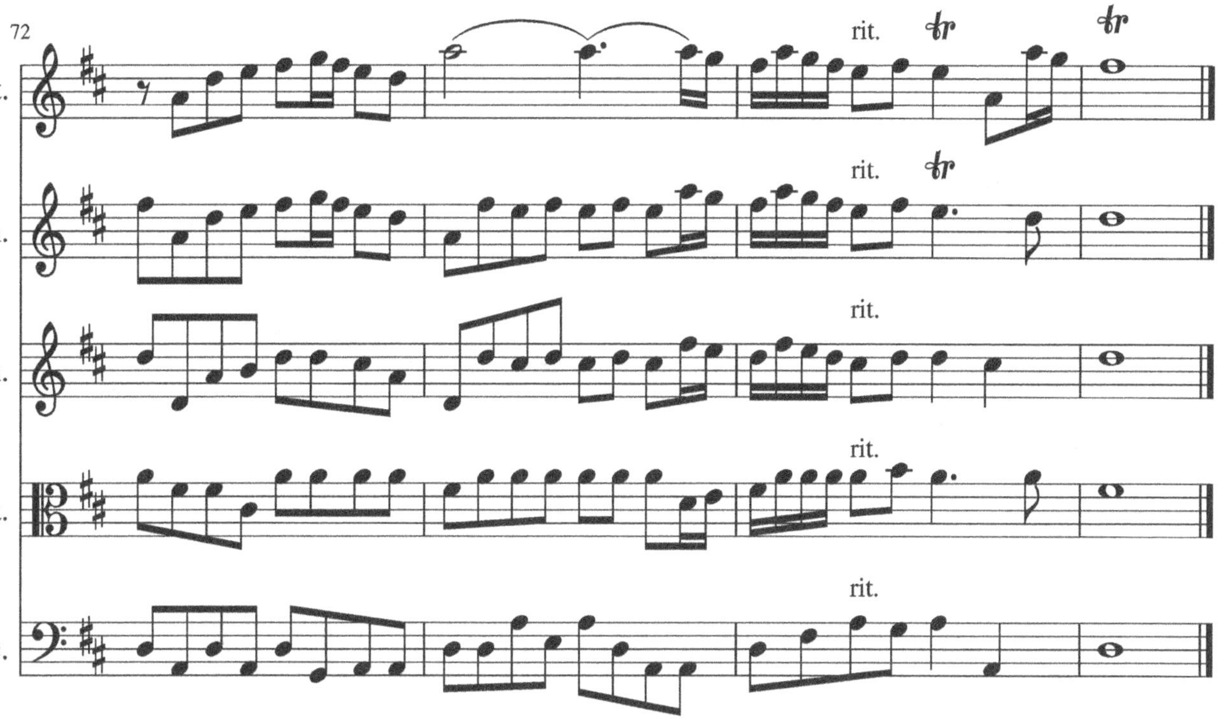
72
C Tpt.
Vln.
Vln.
Vla.
Vc.
rit.
rit.
rit.
rit.
rit.
tr
tr
tr

II.

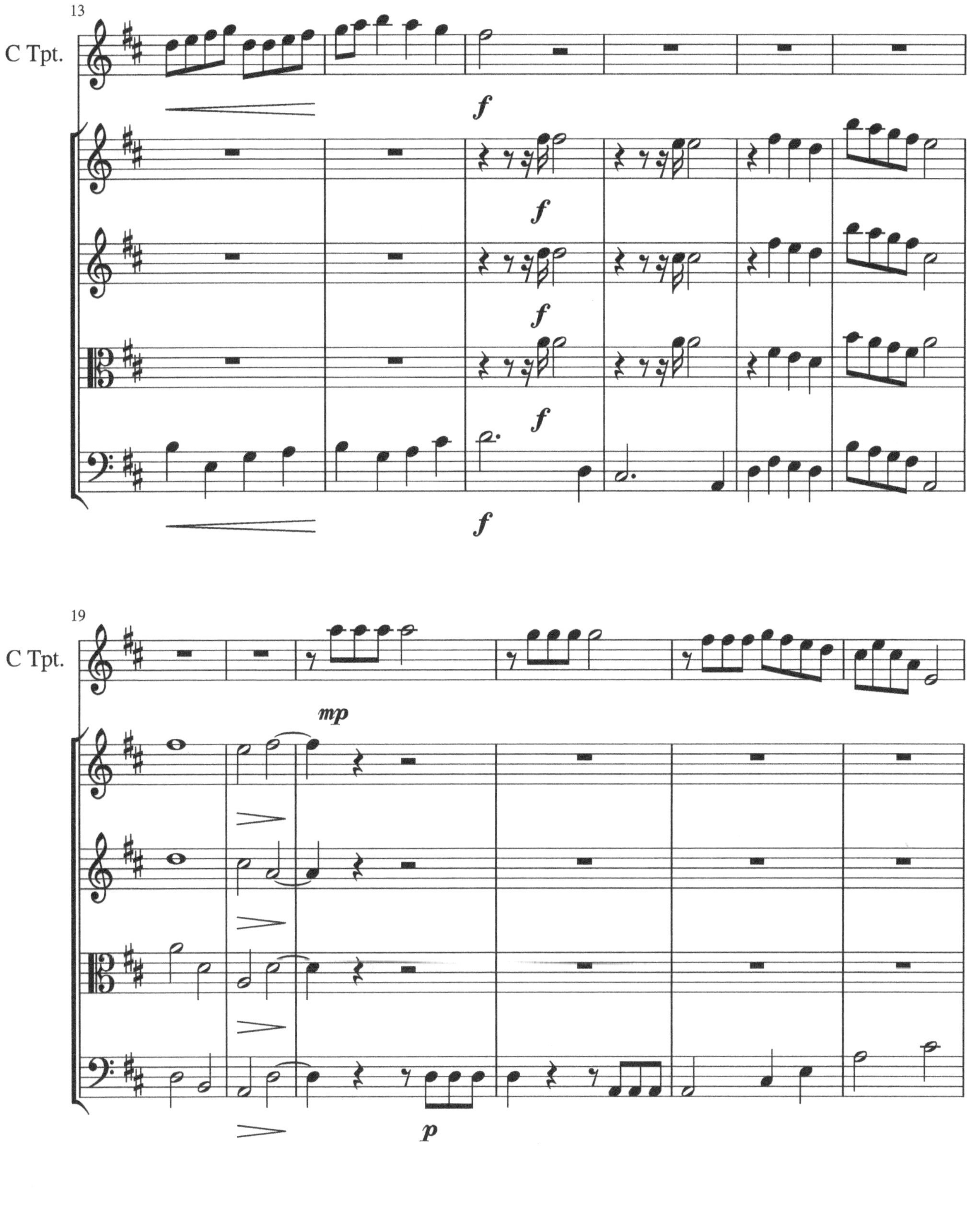
13
C Tpt.
f
f
f
f
f
19
C Tpt.
mp
p

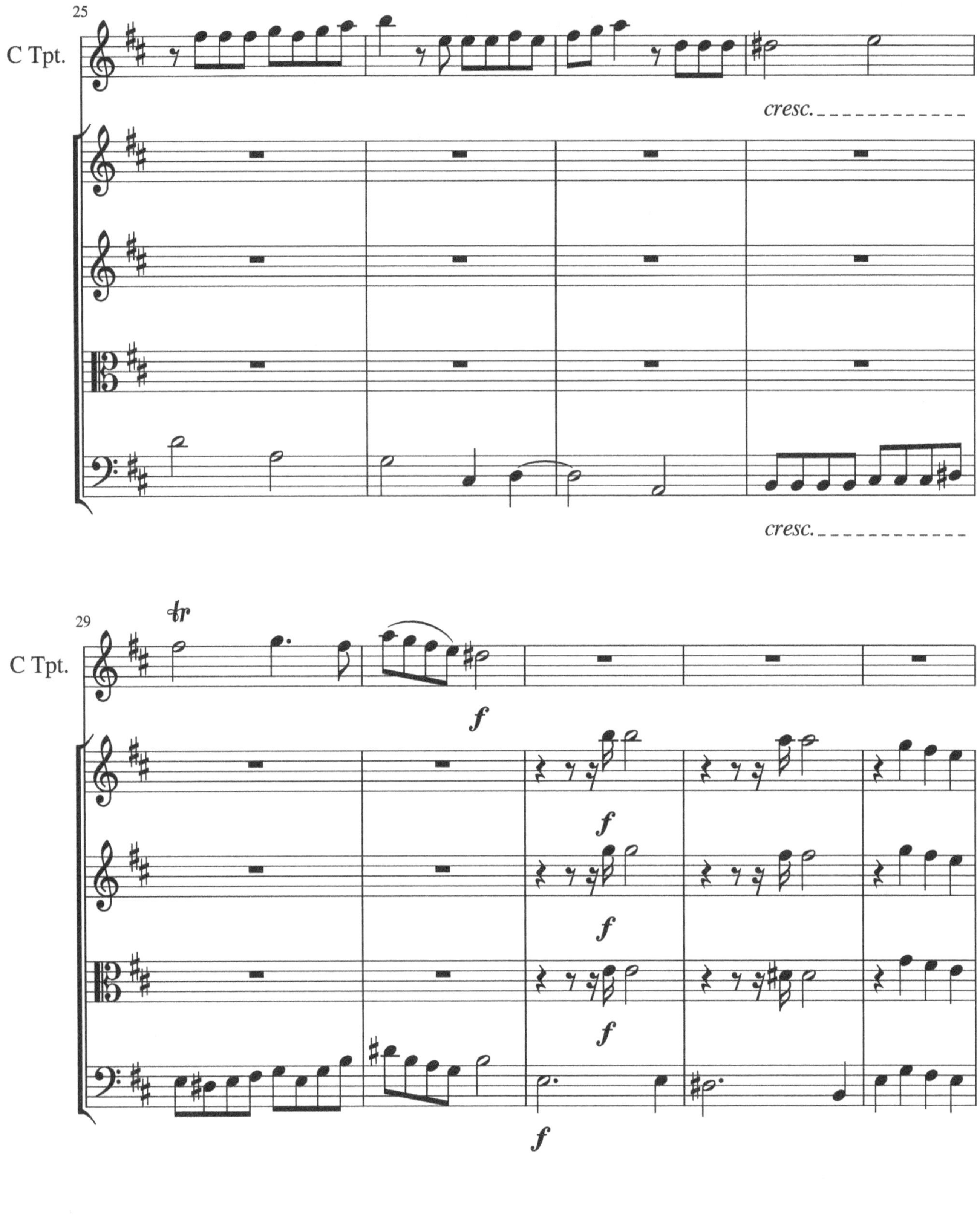
25
C Tpt.
cresc.
cresc.
29
tr
C Tpt.
f
f
f
f
f

167

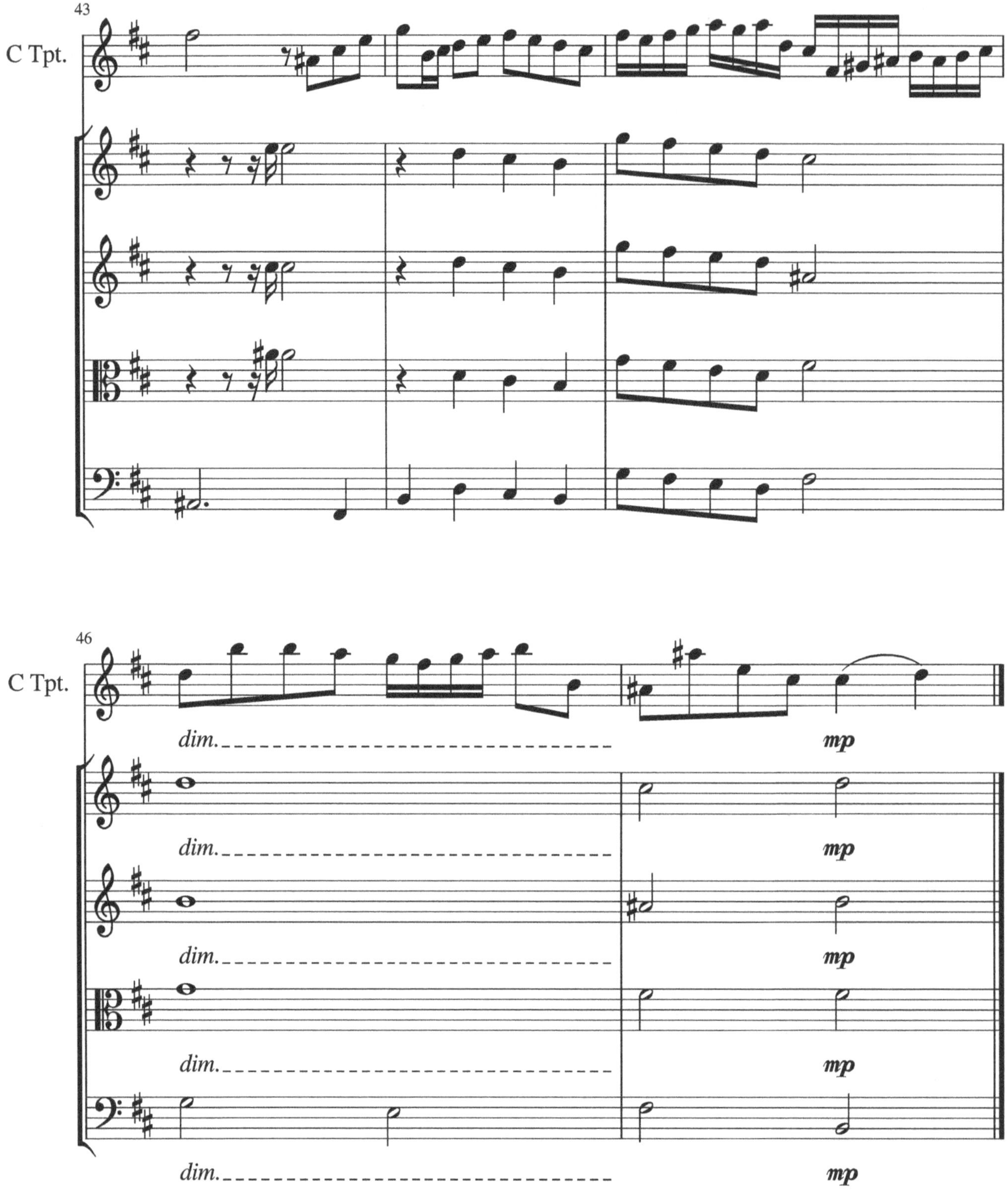

III.

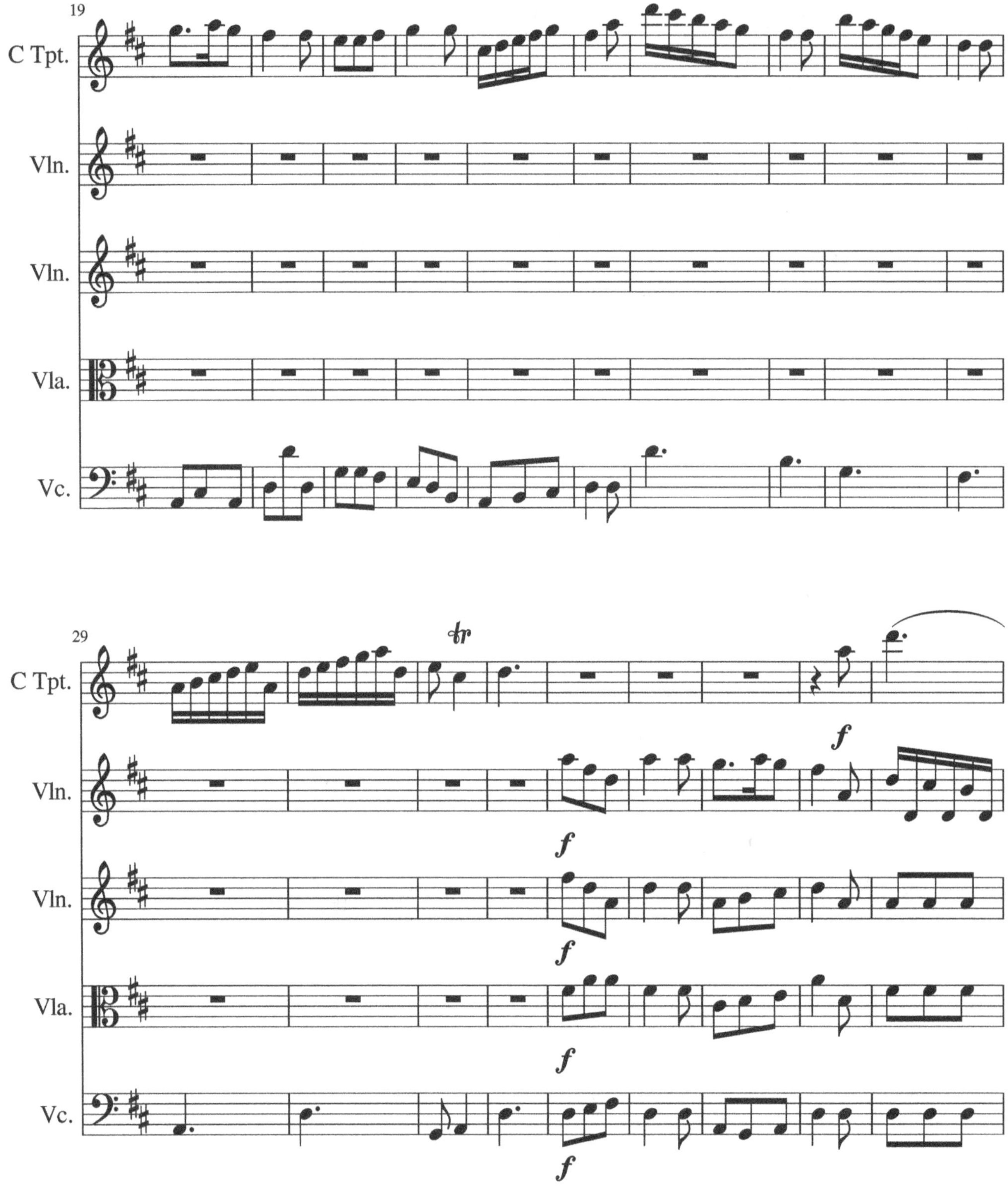
19
C Tpt.
Vln.
Vln.
Vla.
Vc.
29
C Tpt.
tr
f
Vln.
f
Vln.
f
Vla.
f
Vc.
f

38
C Tpt.
Vln.
Vln.
Vla.
Vc.
tr
tr
mf
tr
mf

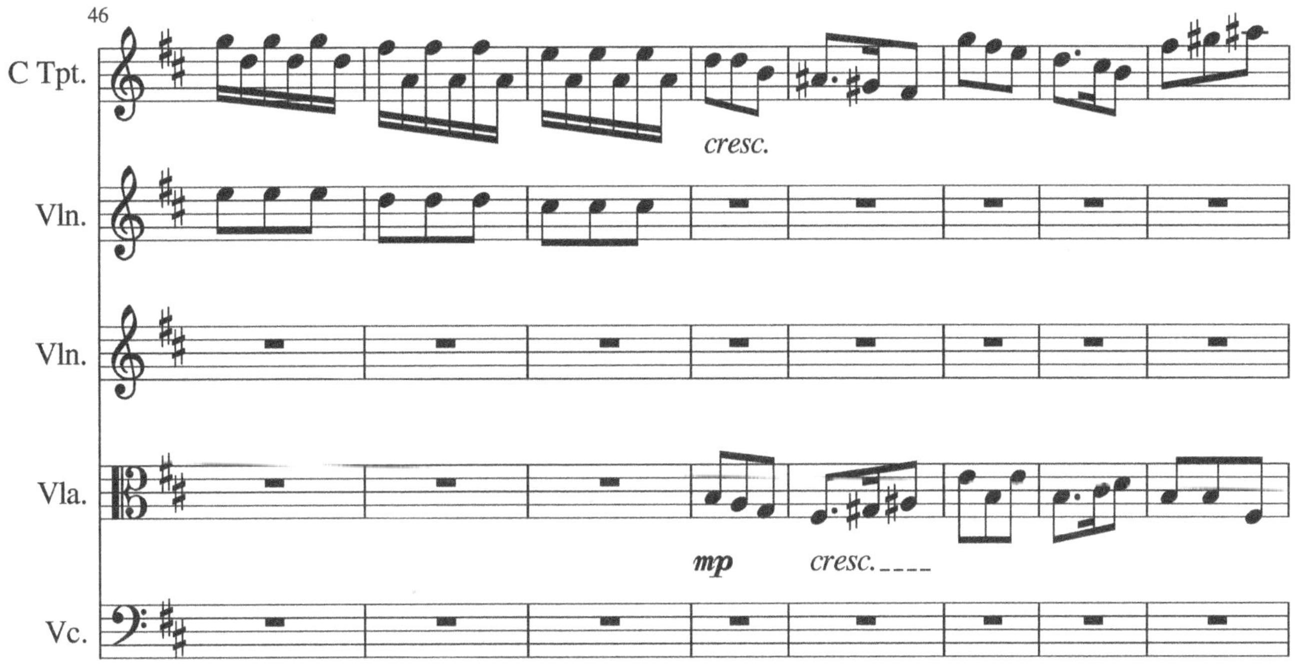
46
C Tpt.
Vln.
Vln.
Vla.
Vc.
cresc.
mp
cresc.

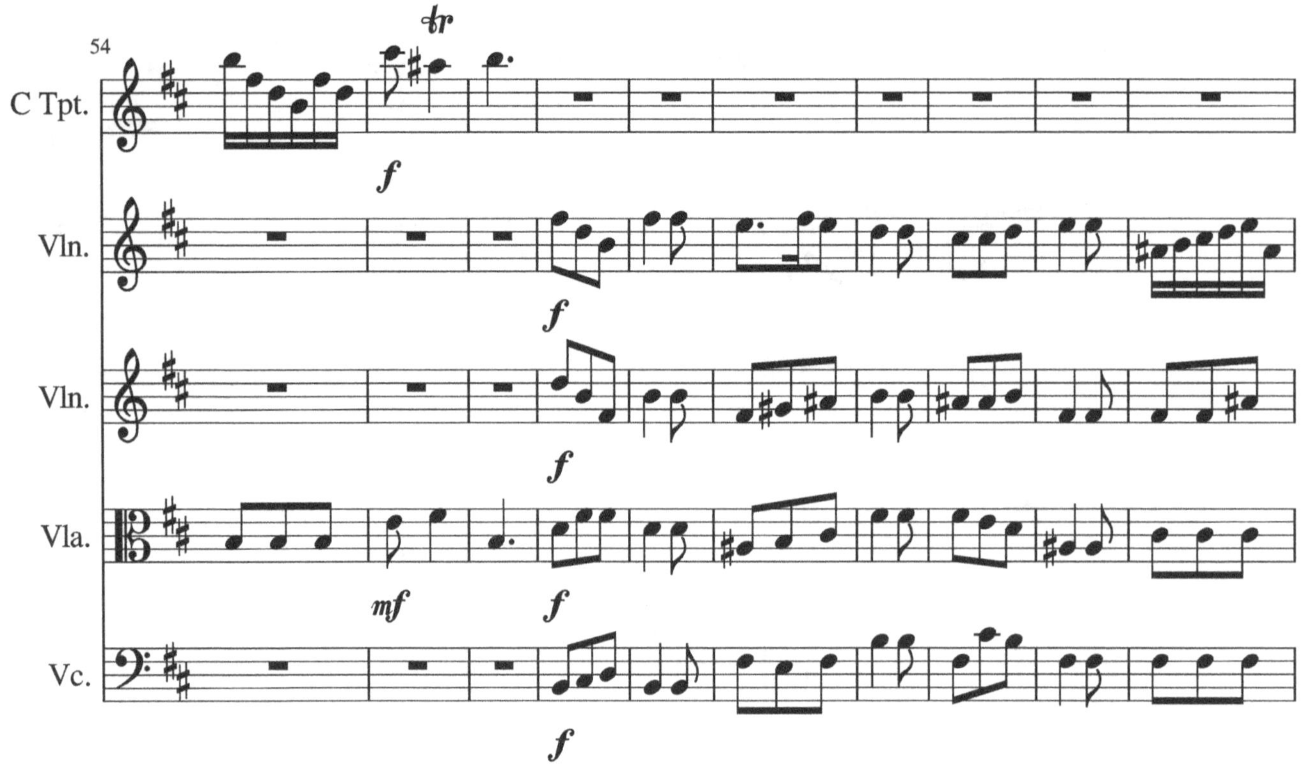
54
C Tpt.
Vln.
Vln.
Vla.
Vc.
tr
f
f
f
mf
f
f

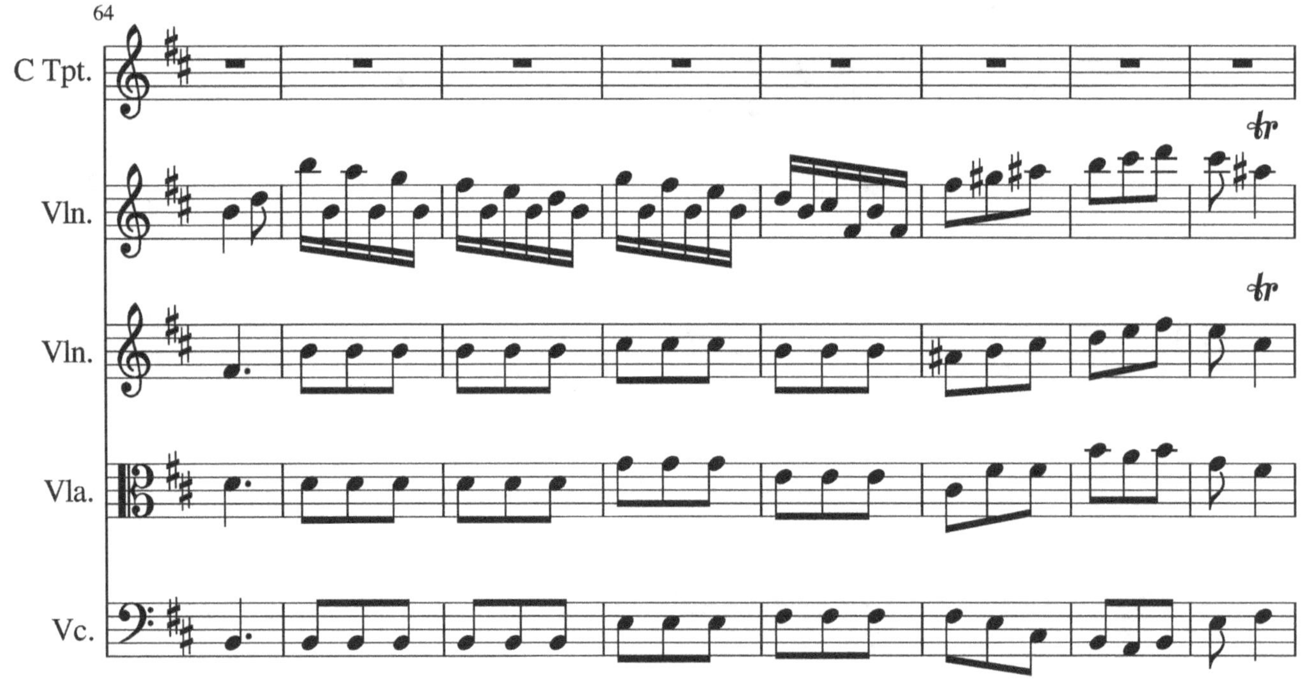
64
C Tpt.
Vln.
Vln.
Vla.
Vc.
tr
tr

72
C Tpt.
Vln.
Vln.
Vla.
Vc.
mf
mp
mp
mp
mp
tr
tr
tr
81
C Tpt.
Vln.
Vln.
Vla.
Vc.
f
f
f
f
f

87
C Tpt.
Vln.
Vln.
Vla.
Vc.
tr
tr
tr

97
C Tpt.
Vln.
Vln.
Vla.
Vc.
tr
cresc.
cresc.
cresc.
cresc.
cresc.

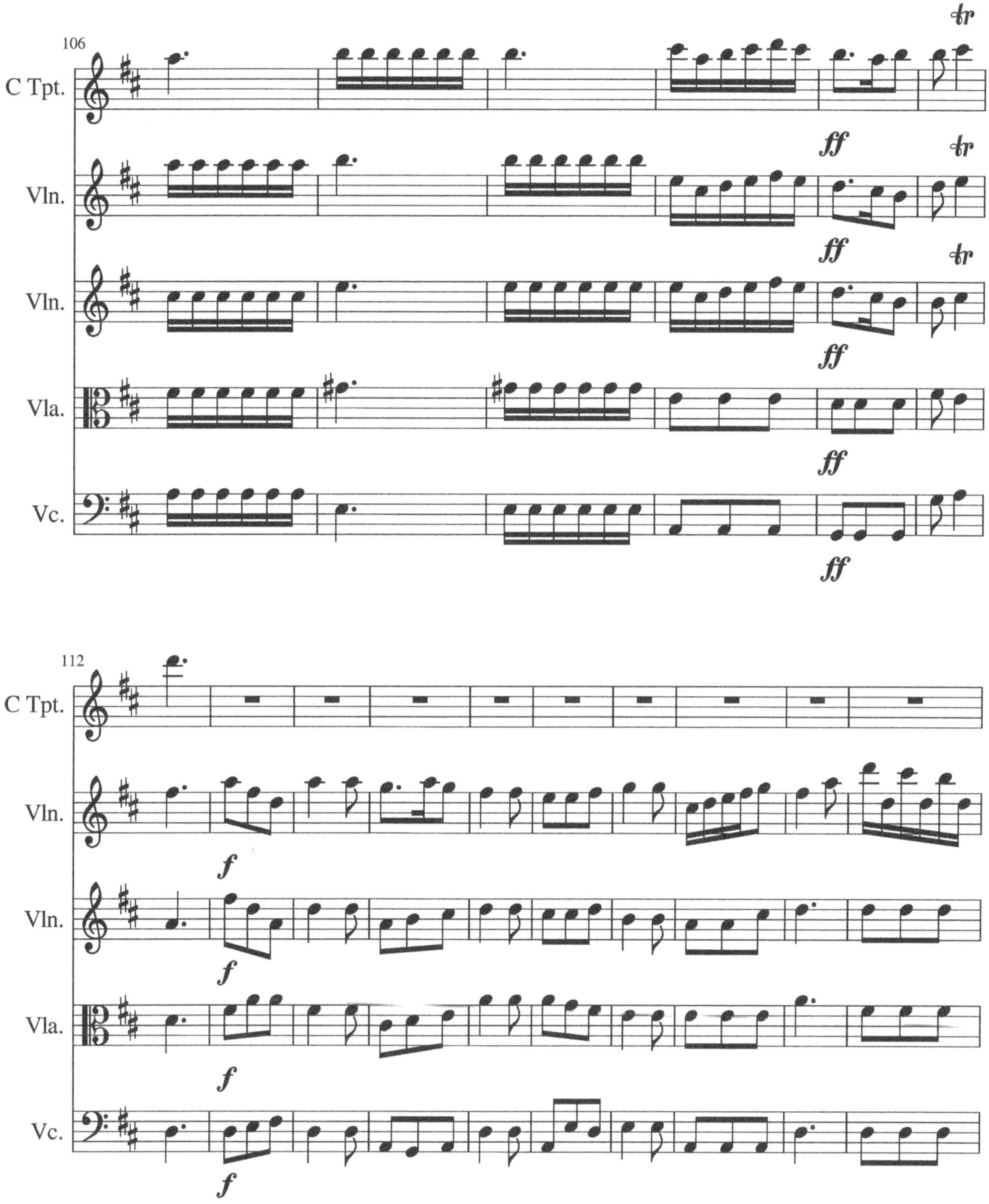
106
C Tpt.
Vln.
Vln.
Vla.
Vc.
tr
ff
112
f

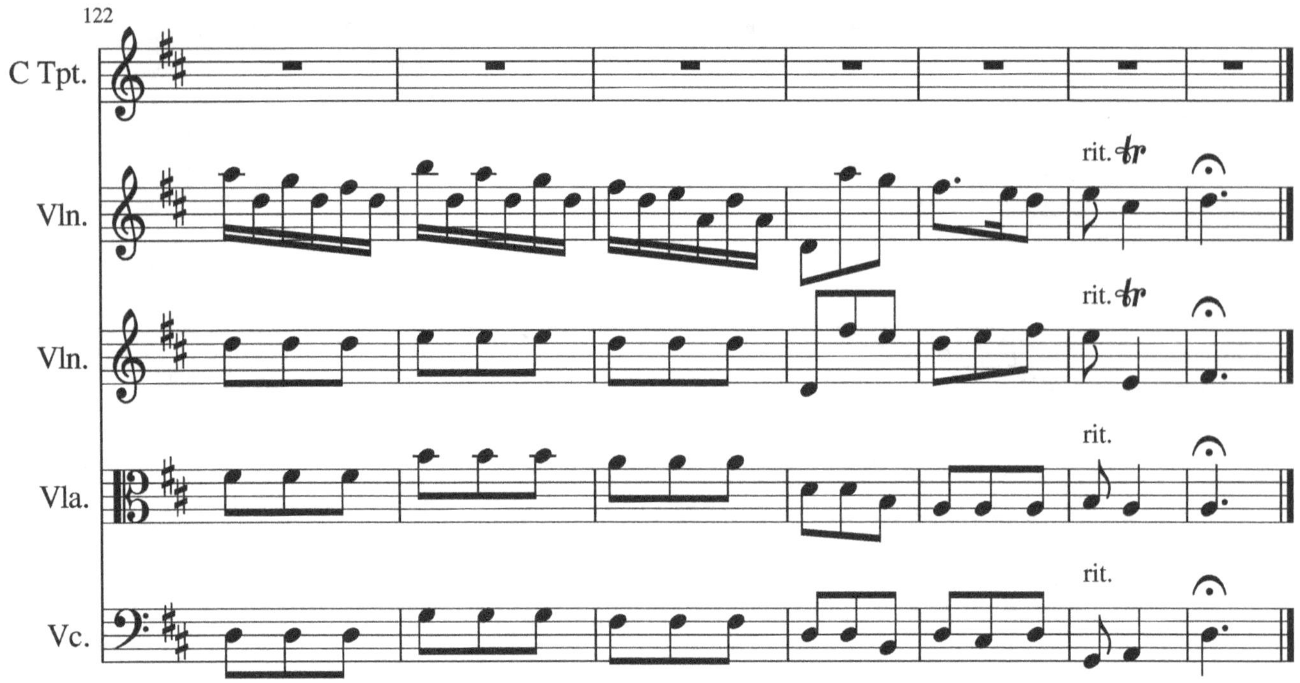
122
C Tpt.
Vln.
Vln.
Vla.
Vc.
rit.
rit.
rit.
rit.

Texts of the Poems

Sunset

H. P. Lovecraft

The cloudless day is richer at its close;
 A golden glory settles on the lea;
Soft, stealing shadows hint of cool repose
  To mellowing landscape, and to calming sea.

And in that nobler, gentler, lovelier light,
 The soul to sweeter, loftier bliss inclines;
Freed from the noonday glare, the favour'd sight
  Increasing grace in earth and sky divines.

But ere the purest radiance crowns the green,
 Or fairest lustre fills th' expectant grove,
The twilight thickens, and the fleeting scene
  Leaves but a hallow'd memory of love!

Ecstasy

Clark Ashton Smith

Blind with your softly fallen hair,
I turn me from the twilight air;
And, ah, the wordless tale of love
My lips upon your lips declare!

High stars are on the shadowy south—
Unseen, unknown: the urgent drouth
Of desolate years in one deep kiss
Would drain the sweetness of your mouth.
Our straining arms that clasp and close

Ache with an ecstasy that grows,
And passion in our secret veins,
Like burning amber, glows and glows.

This love is sweet to have and hold,
Better than sandalwood or gold,
After the barren, bitter loves,
The mad and mournful loves of old.

This love is fortunate and fair,
Behind its veil of fallen hair;
This love has soft and clinging arms,
And a kind bosom, warm and bare.

To Helen

Edgar Allan Poe

Helen, thy beauty is to me
    Like those Nicéan barks of yore,
That gently, o'er a perfumed sea,
    The weary, way-worn wanderer bore
      To his own native shore.

On desperate seas long wont to roam,
    Thy hyacinth hair, thy classic face,
Thy Naiad airs have brought me home
    To the glory that was Greece,
      And the grandeur that was Rome.

Lo! in yon brilliant window-niche
    How statue-like I see thee stand,
    The agate lamp within thy hand!
Ah, Psyche, from the regions which
      Are Holy-Land!

Continuity

H. P. Lovecraft

There is in certain ancient things a trace
Of some dim essence—more than form or weight;
A tenuous aether, indeterminate,
Yet linked with all the laws of time and space.
A faint, veiled sign of continuities
That outward eyes can never quite descry;
Of locked dimensions harbouring years gone by,
And out of reach except for hidden keys.

It moves me most when slanting sunbeams glow
On old farm buildings set against a hill,
And paint with life the shapes which linger still
From centuries less a dream than this we know.
In that strange light I feel I am not far
From the fixt mass whose sides the ages are.

Non Sum Qualis Eram Bonae sub Regno Cynarae

Ernest Dowson

Last night, ah, yesternight, betwixt her lips and mine
There fell thy shadow, Cynara! thy breath was shed
Upon my soul between the kisses and the wine;
And I was desolate and sick of an old passion,
    Yea, I was desolate and bowed my head:
I have been faithful to thee, Cynara! in my fashion.

All night upon mine heart I felt her warm heart beat,
Night-long within mine arms in love and sleep she lay;
Surely the kisses of her bought red mouth were sweet;
But I was desolate and sick of an old passion,
    When I awoke and found the dawn was gray:
I have been faithful to thee, Cynara! in my fashion.

I have forgot much, Cynara! gone with the wind,
Flung roses, roses riotously with the throng,
Dancing, to put thy pale, lost lilies out of mind;
But I was desolate and sick of an old passion,
    Yea, all the time, because the dance was long:
I have been faithful to thee, Cynara! in my fashion.

I cried for madder music and for stronger wine,
But when the feast is finished and the lamps expire,
Then falls thy shadow, Cynara! the night is thine;
And I am desolate and sick of an old passion,
    Yea, hungry for the lips of my desire:
I have been faithful to thee, Cynara! in my fashion.

Ever of You

George Sterling

Ever of you, with heart your heart unfolding,
Ever of you, as Love our fate is molding,
Ever of you, whose love has no withholding,
    Are all my dreams.

Under the fire of silent planets burning,
Under the snows of cloudy dawns returning,
Under the quiet noons that know my yearning,
    I clasp my dreams.

Ever of you, in beauty unforsaking,
Ever of you, for touch of tears awaking,
Ever of you, although the heart be breaking,
    Are all my dreams.

Expectancy

H. P. Lovecraft

I cannot tell why some things hold for me
A sense of unplumbed marvels to befall,
Or of a rift in the horizon's wall
Opening to worlds where only gods can be.
There is a breathless, vague expectancy,
As of vast ancient pomps I half recall,
Or wild adventures, uncorporeal,
Ecstasy-fraught, and as a day-dream free.

It is in sunsets and strange city spires,
Old villages and woods and misty downs,
South winds, the sea, low hills, and lighted towns,
Old gardens, half-heard songs, and the moon's fires.
But though its lure alone makes life worth living,
None gains or guesses what it hints at giving.

My Swan Song

George Sterling

Has man the right
To die and disappear,
When he has lost the fight?
To sever without fear
The irksome bonds of life,
When he is tired of strife?
May he not seek, if it seems best,
Relief from grief? May he not rest
From labors vain, from hopeless task?
—I do not know; I merely ask.

Or must he carry on
The struggle, till it's done?
Will he be damned, if he,
World-weary, tired and ill,

Deprived of strength and will,
Decides he must be free?
Is punishment awaiting those,
Who quit, before the whistle blows,
Who leave behind unfinished task?
—I do not know; I merely ask.

Background

H. P. Lovecraft

I never can be tied to raw, new things,
For I first saw the light in an old town,
Where from my window huddled roofs sloped down
To a quaint harbour rich with visionings.
Streets with carved doorways where the sunset beams
Flooded old fanlights and small window-panes,
And Georgian steeples topped with gilded vanes—
These were the sights that shaped my childhood dreams.

Such treasures, left from times of cautious leaven,
Cannot but loose the hold of flimsier wraiths
That flit with shifting ways and muddled faiths
Across the changeless walls of earth and heaven.
They cut the moment's thongs and leave me free
To stand alone before eternity.

Requiescat

Clark Ashton Smith

What was Love's worth,
Who lived with roses?—
Love that is earth,
And with earth reposes!

What was Love's wonder?—
Scent of the flowers
After the thunder,
Thunder, and showers!

What were the breathless
Words that he said?—
Love that was deathless,
Love that is dead! . . .

Echo hath taken
The song, and flown;
None shall awaken
Music and moan.

Buds and the flower,
All that Love found,
Last but an hour,
Strewn on his mound.

To Science

George Sterling

And if thou slay Him, shall the ghost not rise?
    Yea! if thou conquer Him thine enemy,
    His specter from the dark shall visit thee—
Invincible, necessitous and wise.
The tyrant and mirage of human eyes,
    Exhaled upon the spirit's darkened sea,
    Shares He thy moment of eternity,
Thy truth confronted ever with His lies.

Thy banners gleam a little, and are furled;
    Against thy turrets surge His phantom tow'rs;
        Drugged with His opiates the nations nod,
    Refusing still the beauty of thine hours;
And fragile is thy tenure of this world
        Still haunted by the monstrous ghost of God.

Little Sam Perkins

H. P. Lovecraft

The ancient garden seems tonight
    A deeper gloom to bear,
As if some silent shadow's blight
    Were hov'ring in the air.

With hidden griefs the grasses sway,
    Unable quite to word them—
Remembering from yesterday
    The little paws that stirr'd them.

A Dirge of Victory

Lord Dunsany

Lift not thy trumpet, Victory, to the sky,
　　Nor through battalions nor by batteries blow,
　　But over hollows full of old wire go,
Where, among dregs of war, the long-dead lie
With wasted iron that the guns passed by
　　When they went eastward like a tide at flow;
　　There blow thy trumpet that the dead may know,
Who waited for thy coming, Victory.

It is not we that have deserved thy wreath.
　　They waited there among the towering weeds:
The deep mud burned under the thermite's breath,
　　And winter cracked the bones that no man heeds:
Hundreds of nights flamed by: the seasons passed.
And thou hast come to them at last, at last!

Imprisoned

Mary Krawczak Wilson

You cannot climb too high;
The fortress is made of steel,
Its windows are black and sealed,
And its walls are steeped in lye.

How do you emerge from hell?
Where is the exit to flee?
You scream out: "Let me be free!"
Echoes die in a dark cell.

The floor is icy and cold;
Hissing winds shatter your ears
And magnify every fear
Until your young soul grows old.

You yearn for rays of sunlight,
Yet only charred dust prevails;
It covers your face so pale—
Eyes blinded—you die from fright.

www.ingramcontent.com/pod-product-compliance
Lightning Source LLC
Chambersburg PA
CBHW081149090426
42736CB00017B/3245